My Little
Encyclopedia of
Animals

A DORLING KINDERSLEY BOOK

LONDON, NEW YORK,
MELBOURNE, MUNICH, and DELHI

Author Penelope Arlon
Senior Art Editor Tory Gordon-Harris
Consultant Kim Dennis-Bryan PhD. FZS
Design Assistance Amy McSimpson
Publishing Manager Sue Leonard
Managing Art Editor Clare Shedden
Picture Researcher Sarah Pownall
Production Controller Angela Graef
Jacket Designer Hedi Gutt
Jacket Editor Mariza O'Keeffe

First published in Great Britain in 2004
as Animal Encyclopedia
This edition first published in 2006 by
Dorling Kindersley Limited
80 Strand, London WC2R 0RL

Copyright © 2004, 2006 Dorling Kindersley Limited
A Penguin Company

2 4 6 8 10 9 7 5 3 1
DD374 – 10/06

A CIP catalogue record for this book
is available from the British Lib

ISBN 978-1-4053-1898-3

Colour reproduction by Colourscan, Singapore
Printed and bound in China by Hung Hing

Discover more at
www.dk.com

Contents

Introduction

Mammals

Birds

This book will ask you questions at the bottom of each page...

About this book

The pages of this book have special features that will show you how to get your hands on as much information as possible! Look out for these:

The animal quiz will get you searching through the section for the answers.

Become-an-expert buttons tell you where to look for more information on each subject.

Every page is colour coded to show you which section it is in.

These buttons give extra weird and wonderful animal facts.

The animal kingdom

The animal kingdom is divided into vertebrates and invertebrates. Mammals, birds, reptiles, amphibians, and fish are vertebrates. The invertebrates are in the creepy crawly section.

Animals

All animals have one thing in common – they eat other living things, either plants, animals, or both. Also almost all, except a few sea animals, can move around.

Bird skeleton

The beetle has muscles attached to its skeleton just like you do. Its skeleton is on the outside, however, while yours is on the inside.

Beetle skeleton

Not all birds can fly, although all of them have wings

What is an invertebrate?

The word invertebrate simply means not having a backbone. The "creepy crawly" section of this book is made up of the animals called invertebrates. Some of them have skeletons on the outside of their bodies, some don't have any bones at all.

What is a vertebrate?

Most of the large animals in the world are vertebrates. This means that they have a backbone, and most are made up of bones put together to make a skeleton. Mammals, birds, reptiles, amphibians, and fish are all vertebrates.

Do all animals have brains?

Creepy crawlies

Creepy crawlies, or invertebrates, make up over 95% of all animals. But most of them are so small you don't notice them.

Some people think that there are millions of creepy crawlies we do not even know about yet.

Stag beetle

Ants are insects, which are creepy crawlies.

Ants

Most vertebrates can move around

Vertebrates

All vertebrates came from the same ancestor millions of years ago, but have changed, or evolved, into these four main groups.

Mammals: most live on land, none can breathe underwater.

Birds: all birds have wings and most of them can fly.

Fish: all fish live in the sea or in fresh water.

Reptiles and amphibians: these animals live on land or in water.

Lion

The lion is one of the most ferocious meat-eaters of the mammal group.

Lions keep their sharp claws inside their toes to protect them, until they need to attack.

No, a few invertebrates have no brains.

Mammals

You may wonder if animals such as dogs, bats, elephants, and mice have anything in common. They do – they are all mammals and have more in common than you may think.

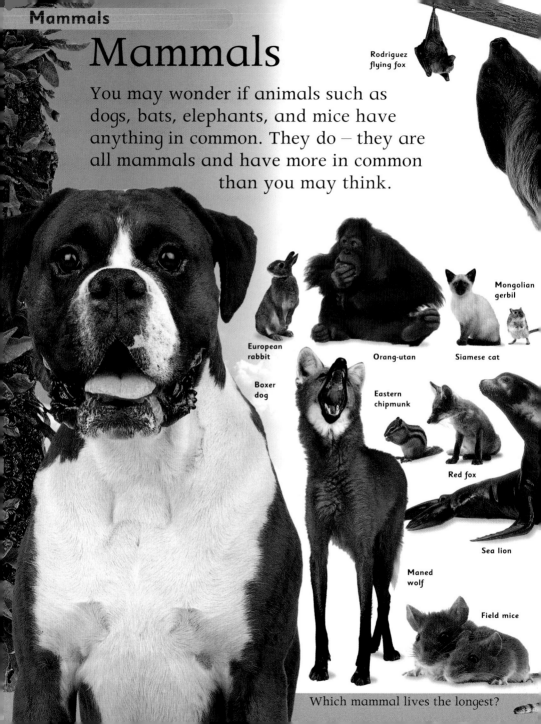

Rodriguez flying fox

European rabbit

Boxer dog

Orang-utan

Eastern chipmunk

Mongolian gerbil

Siamese cat

Red fox

Sea lion

Maned wolf

Field mice

Which mammal lives the longest?

Long-eared bats

Two-toed sloth

Common bat

Animal quiz

Take a look through the Mammals section and see if you can spot who these hairy skins belong to.

Junior mammals

Mammal babies look like little versions of their parents. They are all looked after by their mothers or both parents until they can feed and look after themselves.

Baby red-necked wallaby

Baby tiger

Become an expert...
on the cat family, pages **14-17**
on bats, pages **30-31**

7

The human lives longer than any other mammal.

The world of mammals

Mammals include animals such as the whale, the kangaroo, and you and me! We all have fur, we are warm blooded, and we feed new babies our milk.

Gorilla skeleton

The skeleton

Mammals may look very different, but stripped back to the bone, we all have the basic bony skeleton. Scientists call us vertebrates – animals with a backbone.

Feeding babies

All female mammals produce milk from their bodies that they feed to their babies; this feeding is called suckling. The milk is rich and helps the babies to grow.

Mammal babies

Most mammal females give birth to live babies, rather than laying eggs. The baby grows inside the mother's body until it is born.

Become an expert...

on bears, pages 20-21
on elephants, pages 34-35

Baby gorilla

Within the mammal group there are many different families.

This baby gorilla is a member of the primate family.

How many mammal families are there?

Polar bears can live in chilly Arctic regions because they are warm blooded and have thick fur.

Hairy beasts

All mammals are hairy – some are much hairier than others – and most have hair, often called fur, all over their bodies. They are hairy to keep them warm.

Elephant

This elephant may not look hairy but it does have hair on its body.

Warm blood

Mammals are warm blooded, which means they can warm up and cool down their bodies to keep their temperature level. An elephant in the hot jungle is the same temperature as a polar bear in the snow.

Polar bear

Getting around

Mammals are many different shapes that

Cats: some mammals, such as the cat, have long legs to run with.

Bats: the bat is the only mammal that can fly – it has wings.

Dolphins: sea mammals have flippers and strong tails to swim with.

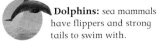

Moles: the mole has feet like spades, which are useful for burrowing.

The polar bear has thick fur all over its body.

The odd one out

It is usually true that animals give birth to live babies, but there are a few species, including this duck-billed platypus, that lay eggs. Platypus eggs are soft and the size of marbles.

9

Lemurs and monkeys

Monkeys and lemurs, along with the apes, make up the mammal group known as primates.

Howler monkey

The loudest land animal on Earth

Talking to each other is important to primates, which live together in large groups. This howler monkey screams to neighbouring groups and can be heard several miles away.

The emperor tamarin has a long, white moustache.

Ring-tailed lemur

Lemurs

Lemurs are found only on the island of Madagascar, in the Indian Ocean. They have thin bodies and often move by jumping along on their back legs. Sitting upright with its hands on its knees, this ring-tailed lemur is sunbathing.

Monkey business

Most people think monkeys all look similar, but some are quite different.

White-faced saki: the male is black and the female brown.

Tamarin: the golden lion tamarin has gold fur and a long mane.

Woolly monkey: it lives in South America and has thick fur.

Proboscis monkey: this male monkey has a very long, prominent nose.

Monkeys

Monkeys have grasping hands so they can climb trees. Many have recognizable features, like this tamarin's white moustache.

weird or what?

Japanese macaques, a type of monkey, live in the mountains of northern Japan. To keep warm in the winter, they take baths in the hot volcanic springs.

Which are longer, a monkey's arms or legs?

Treetops

All monkeys are excellent climbers – some have long tails that they use as another limb. The spider monkey's tail is bald at the end for extra grip.

Spider monkeys have no thumbs

Monkeys have hands like ours that can grasp branches.

Mandrill

Ground monkey

The mandrill is one of the few monkeys that only climbs trees to sleep at night. During the day, it walks around on all fours. When a male feels threatened, it yawns widely revealing its fearsome teeth.

Woolly spider monkey

Bushbaby

Bushbaby

The bushbaby is a small primate that sleeps during the day and ventures out to hunt at night. It has huge eyes that help it to see in the dark.

A monkey's arms are longer than its legs.

The apes

Many people confuse monkeys and apes. Apes are large, intelligent creatures that have no visible tails and can stand more upright than monkeys. You and I are members of the ape family.

The mighty gorilla

Gorillas are the largest and most powerful of the ape family, but they are not aggressive. They live in forests in central Africa.

Gorilla

Family life

Gorillas live in groups of up to 40 animals, which consist of one male and many females and babies. The males are twice the size of the females and as they mature they grow a strip of silvery fur across their backs.

What is the dominant male gorilla in its group called?

King of the swingers

Gibbons are the most agile of all the apes. Their wrists and shoulders are very flexible, which means they are able to swing from branch to branch quickly. They live in pairs.

Treetop apes

These orange orang-utans live in the rainforests of Borneo and Sumatra up in the trees. They rarely go down to the jungle floor, preferring to eat and sleep in the treetops.

The clever chimp

Chimpanzees are very intelligent indeed. They communicate with facial expressions and are one of the only animals to use tools.

This chimp is breaking nut shells using a piece of stone as a tool.

Grooming strengthens friendships within the group.

Grooming

Chimps live in communities of up to 120 apes. Grooming is very important in ape societies. They can often be seen picking dirt and ticks out of each other's fur.

The dominant male is known as a "silverback".

Lynx

The cat family

All cats around the world spend their time doing the same sorts of activities: hunting, eating, and sleeping.

This lynx is about twice the size of a pet cat.

Living alone

Cats like to live on their own; very few live in groups. The only cats that live together are mothers and their babies.

Cat carnivores

Cats eat only meat, and those that live in the wild have to catch it. Some are fussier than others.

Caracal: these cats can leap high into the air to catch birds.

Bobcat: this cat lives in the woodlands of North America and eats rabbits.

Jaguarundi: this small, stocky cat eats anything it can catch.

Fishing cat: this cat catches fish by grabbing them with its claws.

Pumas are the long jumpers of the cat world. They can make massive leaps of 12 m (40 ft).

Climbers

Some cats live in forests and all cats can climb trees. They have very good balance and razor sharp claws that hook into branches.

Puma

Why do cats lick their fur?

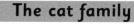

The loudest roar

Most big cats roar; when this lion gets angry, his roar can be heard 8 km (5 miles) away! All other cats miaow, purr, and growl.

Lion

There are more than 300 million pet cats in the world. They are closely related to wild cats.

Domestic cat

A fine coat

A cat's fur keeps it warm and camouflaged. Cats spend a lot of time licking their fur with their rough tongues to clean it.

Cat features

All cats look similar, but their coats, shapes, and sizes are suited to where they live. This serval has a long neck and big ears to enable it to see and hear well in long grass.

Stalk and pounce

Unlike dogs, cats cannot run fast for long distances, so they rely on their ability to stalk and pounce. When stalking, they keep their bodies low, move slowly, and then pounce.

Serval

Ocelot

Become an expert...

on dogs that live in the wild, pages **18-19**

The ocelot is now a protected species as many were killed for their fur.

Cats lick their fur to clean themselves and to keep cool.

Big cats

The five largest, most ferocious meat eaters of the cat family are known as the "big cats". They are the lion, tiger, jaguar, leopard, and snow leopard.

Black leopard

Leopards come in different colours, but most are yellow with black spots. Black panthers were once thought to be a different type of cat, but are actually black leopards.

King of the cats

Lions, found on the grassy plains of Africa, are the only cats that live in groups, or prides.

All mother cats carry their cubs in their mouths.

Sleepy heads

Cats are officially the sleepiest animals in the world: they spend over 19 hours a day asleep. Prides, of lions can often be seen napping under trees. They are perfectly safe to sleep in the open as they are not in danger of being killed by another animal.

Pride of lions

Why do cats have whiskers?

Water cat

The jaguar has large spots and loves swimming, which is quite unusual among cats. During the day it catches fish by flipping them out of the water with its paws. At night it hunts for animals in the jungle.

Tiger

Spotted leopard

Leopards love to climb trees. High up in the branches is a good spot to watch what is going on below. Often they will even drag their kill up trees to prevent it being stolen.

Leopard

The giant tiger

Tigers are the largest and most powerful of all the cats – they are 10 times stronger than a man! They live all over Asia from the rainforest to the woodlands of Siberia.

Female lions do not have manes like the males.

Become an expert...

on the fastest land mammal on Earth, the cheetah, pages

154-155

Tigers hunt mainly in the dark.

Their whiskers help them to feel their way in the dark.

17

The dog family

When you think of dogs, you probably think of pets, but many members of the dog family live in the wild.

Wolves

Wolves live in packs of about 20, which are led by a male and female. They are true meat eaters and all work together to hunt and kill. They have very sharp teeth that are useful for tearing up meat.

Training the wolf

Over thousands of years dogs have been trained by people to do certain jobs for them.

Guide dogs: many dogs are used to guide blind people.

Sheep dogs: people have been using dogs to round up sheep for centuries.

Police dogs: these guard dogs use their noses to sniff out criminals.

At night whole packs howl together to warn other wolves that they are there.

European grey wolf

Wolves sometimes spray their urine to mark out their territory.

Wolf language

Facial expressions and body language are used by wolves within a pack to communicate with each other. When they want to keep other wolf packs away, they howl rather than bark.

What is the tail of a fox called?

Urban foxes

The fox is a small dog. It tends to hunt at night and lives alone or in small family groups. Recently the red fox has become a common sight in towns and cities, where it raids dustbins for food.

African hunting dog

When the dogs have killed, the whole pack shares the food.

These dogs are often known as "painted wolves" because of their beautiful colouring.

weird or what?

Dogs have been man's best friend for over 12,000 years! All pet dogs are descendants of the grey wolf and still share many characteristics such as very good smell and hearing.

Red fox

Raccoon dog

This hairy dog is called the raccoon dog, although it is not related to the raccoon. It is one of the only dogs that climbs trees.

Wild dogs

African hunting dogs live in packs of up to 30. They have long legs and a lean body. They hunt together as a pack and can kill prey larger than themselves. They hunt at least once a day.

Grey wolves live in North America and northern Asia. They are about 1 m (3 ft) tall.

A fox's tail is called a brush.

Bears

Members of the bear family are big, furry mammals with large heads, thick legs, and short tails. They have five claws on each foot.

Bear necessities

Bears have a good sense of smell, but weak eyesight and hearing. This is reflected in their large nose and very small ears and eyes.

Brown bear

The brown bear can stand up to 3.5 m (11 ft) tall, that's twice the size of a tall man!

Bear families

There are only eight types of bear in the world, including the polar bear and the brown bear.

Brown bear: this bear is the largest meat-eating mammal on Earth.

Polar bear: the biggest and most deadly bear. It lives in the Arctic.

Spectacled bear: it got this name because it looks as if it is wearing glasses.

A long doze

Many bears are dormant in the winter, which means they doze or sleep non-stop for a long time. They eat and eat during the summer and autumn months to build up fat that they can live off in the winter. Cubs are born during this time.

Which bear makes nests in trees?

American black bear: this bear sleeps up to six months during dormancy.

Sloth bear: it has claws of 8 cm (3 in) that it uses to tear open ant nests.

Giant panda: this black-and-white bear always lives by itself.

Sun bear: it uses its 25 cm (10 in) tongue to suck honey out of trees.

Asiatic black bear: this very rare bear is a protected species.

Climbing bears

Bears normally walk slowly, but if they feel the need they can gallop at very high speeds. It may seem unlikely because of their size, but most bears are also able to climb trees. This giant panda is climbing a bamboo tree to eat the shoots.

The giant panda eats mostly bamboo shoots. It will sometimes eat small animal grubs if it can find them.

Water bears

Polar bears live in the Arctic. They have thick fur to keep them warm in the chilly weather. They are excellent swimmers and can hold their breath for up to two minutes underwater.

Mother love

The mother bear looks after her cubs fiercely during their first year, teaching them how to survive. She sometimes stands on her back legs to increase her size and frighten her enemies away.

The sun bear.

Small and cunning

There are many small, meat-eating mammals that hunt or scavenge for their food. Many are known for their clever hunting methods.

Stoat

Laughing hyenas

At dusk, these sloping-backed mammals emerge to hunt or find dead animals to eat. They live in small groups and make whooping calls that sound like mad laughter.

The weasel family

Members of the weasel family have long bodies and short legs. They have a fierce reputation for hunting – they are able to kill animals larger than themselves.

All year round, the American mink has a dark brown coat and a thin white beard.

Weasel

Stoats

Stoats and minks are small animals related to weasels. In summer stoats are brown with a white tummy and in the winter they turn white so that they are camouflaged in the snow.

Weasels hunt by themselves, killing animals by biting their necks.

Become an expert...

on another relation to the weasel, the badger, page 25

Why are many of the weasel family becoming rare?

Raccoons

Raccoons are small animals with fox-like faces and bandit-style masks. They are inquisitive creatures who make clever hunters.

Raccoons are often seen in towns rifling through dustbins. They have even been known to open door latches.

Smelly skunks

Skunks are found in the Americas and feed on small animals and fruit. When threatened, they lift their tails and let out a foul stink, which you can smell from a kilometre (half a mile) away!

Mongoose family

Mongooses are so cunning that they can kill some of the world's most poisonous animals, such as snakes.

This mongoose has clamped its teeth around a snake's neck to kill it.

Meerkats

Weasel relatives

These mammals belong to the weasel family.

 Wolverine: this animal has a larger, stockier body than a weasel.

Polecat: polecats are sometimes kept as pets. They are called ferrets.

 American mink: it hunts on land and in water.

Meerkats

Meerkats are a type of mongoose that live in groups. They hunt during the day, while a sentry scans the area from the highest point, sitting upright, looking out for enemies.

The burrowers

Many mammals are diggers, building their homes beneath the ground. Some only use their burrows to sleep in, others live underground.

Rabbits

Most rabbits dig burrows, called warrens, underground to protect themselves from enemies, to shelter from cold, and to provide a safe place for their babies. European rabbits live in large groups.

Rabbit warrens are often a maze of tunnels.

Boxing hares

Hares are relatives of rabbits but have longer ears. Males can sometimes be seen boxing each other to win females. They stand on their back legs, hitting out with the front ones.

Hares do not actually live underground, they live in hollows they make with their bodies in the earth.

24

What are rabbit babies called?

The aardvark

This animal has a body like a pig, ears like a rabbit, and it licks up ants like an anteater, but it is not related to any of these animals! It is a very good burrower digging long tunnels with its claws.

Armadillo

Armadillos look as if they could take on an army with their bony armoured backs. They dig burrows to find food and make dens. Most rest in their burrows during the day and hunt by night.

Badgers have quite large, stocky bodies, and small heads with long noses to root out food.

Badgers have poor eyesight but a good sense of smell.

Badgers

Badgers have short legs that are good for scurrying down tunnels. Their burrows, known as setts, are passed down through generations of badgers. They tend to hunt at night.

Moles

You will know when European moles are about because they leave mole hills behind on the ground. Moles spend most of their lives under-ground eating worms and insects.

The star-nosed mole "swims" through the earth, using its paws as paddles.

European mole

Rabbit babies are called kittens.

Insect-eating mammals

Many small mammals spend their lives eating insects and other small creepy crawlies. Most of them only hunt at night.

Scaly anteaters

Sometimes called a scaly anteater, this pangolin is n actually related to anteate: It uses its long claws to dig anthills and termite mound

Pangolins shut their nostrils while eating ants to stop them from rushing up their nose.

The giant anteater

Giant anteaters are large mammals that like to eat ants and termites. They have a large nose and a tongue that is as long as your arm, perfect for sticking into termite mounds.

Silky anteater

The silky anteater has a shorter nose and paler fur than its cousins. It spends much of its time digging out tree ants and licking them up.

The giant anteater can eat more than 30,000 ants in one day!

Become an expert...

on ants and termites, pages **124-125**
on earthworms, page **133**

How big is the smallest shrew?

When curled up the hedgehog looks like a spiny ball.

The head and paws appear as the hedgehog sniffs its surroundings and looks out for danger.

Small and prickly

Hedgehogs use their long noses to snuffle in the earth for insects and worms. They are covered in sharp spines that are made of a kind of hair. If this creature feels threatened it rolls its body into a prickly ball. Not many animals would attempt to eat a spiny hedgehog!

Hedgehog

The hedgehog flips itself over and goes on its way.

Shrews

Shrews are small, active mammals that have to eat a diet of insects and worms every few hours to keep their energy up. They can eat more than their weight in food every day.

The spiny echidna

The insect-eating echidna is also covered in spines. It is one of the most unusual animals because, with the duck-billed platypus, it is one of the only mammals that lays eggs.

Echidna

Shrew senses

A shrew uses its very good senses of smell and hearing to find food, such as small insects and earthworms.

Pygmy shrew

The pygmy white-toothed shrew is half the size of your finger.

Rodents

Rodents are the mammal group that includes mice and rats. Rodents are found all over the world from the desert to the Arctic.

A rat's tail helps it to balance and turn in the water.

The brown rat

The rat is considered a pest. It lives almost everywhere in the world and can exist in huge numbers if enough food is available.

Brown rat

Brown rat

Dinner time

Rats eat everything we eat and more, which is why they can survive worldwide. The brown rat is a very good swimmer and can catch small fish underwater.

Rats and mice have a very good sense of smell and "talk" to each other using their body smells.

weird or what?

The black rat was responsible for killing half of London in 1665. It brought fleas to England that carried a deadly disease called the Black Death.

Rodent teeth

All rodents have four big front teeth, like this marmot's. They are very sharp.

What is the biggest rodent in the world?

Rodent groups

Over 40% of all the mammals in the world are rodents. They come in many shapes and sizes.

Hamster: this creature comes from Western Asia and is a very popular pet.

Squirrel: it is an excellent tree climber and uses its tail for balance.

Vole: water voles live by rivers and lakes and make burrows in the banks.

Naked mole rat: it lives underground and burrows with flat feet.

Porcupine: this animal has sharp spikes that it raises when threatened.

Mice

Mice have pointed noses and long whiskers, which help them find their way around dark corners. This house mouse eats many different types of food and can produce 36,000 droppings in a year.

Harvest mouse

The burrows in the town are connected by long tunnels.

Towns of rodents

Some rodents live on their own, but a lot of them live in large communities, such as these prairie dogs, which live in burrows underground called towns.

Harvest mice use their tails like hands, to grip onto stalks.

A long, long sleep

The dormouse can be found in the woods and fields of Europe and is an excellent climber and jumper. It hibernates, or sleeps, for seven months during the winter without waking up.

House mouse

The capybara, it's as big as a pig!

Flying mammals

Some mammals have "wings" so they can glide through the air, but bats are the only mammals that can actually fly by flapping their wings.

Flying squirrel

Greater mouse-eared bats

During the day bats roost in dark caves, trees, or under a roof of a building. They sleep upside-down.

The glider
The flying squirrel has loose pieces of skin on either side of its body. When it jumps it opens them out like an umbrella and can glide for 100 m (330 ft), steering with its tail and legs.

Bats
Bat's wings are actually long arms with skin stretching between each finger. Their thumbs stick out like small claws to grip branches.

— Claw-like thumb

Bats squeak to find one another in the dark.

Vampire bat

The saliva of vampire bats numbs the skin of its victims so they can't feel the blood-sucking bite.

Bat features
Bats have a variety of head shapes, which reflect their feeding habits.

Fruit bat: has a long snout, and a long tongue to sip nectar and eat fruit.

Long eared bat: this bat has large ears that can hear insects' wings flapping.

Long-nosed bat: these bats have long noses to help them smell flowers.

The real vampire
The vampire bat's favourite meal is fresh blood, even yours! It feeds by digging its sharp teeth into the flesh, then laps up the blood.

What is the smallest bat in the world?

Bat babies

Some bats bring their babies up together in a huge nursery, often filled with thousands of bats. Amazingly the mother can always find her baby when she returns with food.

Fruit bat

Bat diet

Most bats eat insects, others, like this fruit bat, use their long tongues to eat fruit and sip nectar from flowers.

Catching insects

Bats are very good at catching insects in mid-air — in the dark! They find them by making clicking noises and waiting for the echoes to bounce off the insects.

Become an expert...

on gliding frogs, pages 100-101
on bloodsuckers, pages 116-117

This Geoffroy's long-nosed bat drinks nectar.

The Kitti's hog-nosed bat is the smallest — it is the size of a bumble bee.

Marsupials

A marsupial is a mammal with a pocket called a pouch for carrying its babies in.

Koala

Koalas look like little bears. They live in Australia and are the only animal that eats eucalyptus leaves. They are so hard to digest that koalas spend 19 hours of the day sleeping to let their tummies settle.

When the baby koala gets too big for the pouch, it clings to its mother's back instead.

More marsupials

Apart from a few that live in South America, almost all marsupials come from Australasia. They vary a lot in looks.

Dorian's tree kangaroo: this small kangaroo can climb trees.

Numbat: this marsupial has the most teeth of any mammal. It has 52.

Rabbit-eared bandicoot: is a burrower with big ears.

Little devil

The Tasmanian devil is not much bigger than a small dog but is is very aggressive. It is the biggest meat-eating marsupial and has such powerful jaws that it can eat the entire animal – bones and all!

A kangaroo's front legs are

Bouncing marsupials

Kangaroos cannot walk. Instead they have enormous back legs that they use to jump everywhere. They can move very fast just by leaping.

Become an expert...

on a mammal that lays eggs! pages **9, and 27**

32

Which are bigger, wallabies or kangaroos?

Supermum!

Opossums live in the Americas. Unusually for marsupials, the mother has no pouch. Instead her babies cling to her. Sometimes one mother can have up to 20 babies at one time!

Opossums are very good tree climbers.

This joey is definitely big enough to climb out of its pouch.

In the pouch

Most marsupials have pouches. When the babies are born, they are as small as beans and wriggle straight into the pouch. They do most of their growing there, instead of in their mother's tummy.

Little joey

Kangaroo and wallaby babies are commonly known as joeys. They spend several months in the mother's pouch, and even when they are big enough to walk, they sometimes jump back in for safety.

not used when they bounce

Their huge tails help to balance them when they run.

Kangaroos look like wallabies, but they are bigger.

33

The mighty elephant

The elephant is the largest land animal on Earth – the biggest one ever found weighed as much as 150 men! There are two main types of elephant, the African and Asian.

African elephants flap their enormous ears to keep themselves cool in the hot sun.

African elephants

Living in herds

African elephants live in groups called herds. However, only females and youngsters live together, males live on their own. A family usually contains about 8-10 elephants.

Elephants' tusks are very big upper teeth.

Playtime!
Baby elephants love to play, which is an important part of growing up in a herd. They chase one another, throw sticks, and climb all over each other.

How big is an elephant's toenail?

An amazing nose

Elephants have enormous noses, called trunks. But they are no ordinary noses, they do many more jobs than simply smelling. Elephants use their trunks to eat, drink, wash, and even pick up vibrations on the ground.

Elephants make loud, trumpeting calls to each other.

Asian elephant

Elephants use their trunks to grab leaves high up in the trees that other animals cannot reach.

A handy nose

An elephant can grip at the end of its nose, just like your hand. It uses its trunk to grasp plants and eat them, to greet other elephants, and to show aggression to others.

Bathtime!

An elephant's skin is very sensitive and needs a lot of bathing to rinse away creepy crawlies and keep it cool. It often sucks up water in its trunk and sprays it over its body.

African elephants have much bigger ears than Asian elephants

An elephant's toenail is as big as your hand!

On the hoof

A hoof is a certain type of foot with a hard covering. Hoofed mammals are found all over the world.

Different hoofs

A hoofed foot has a hard case, like a big toenail, around each toe for protection. Hoofed feet make fast runners.

Horse: a horse has only one toe surrounded by a hoof. It runs on its tiptoes.

Rhinoceros: these large hoofed mammals have three toes.

Camel: the camel has two toes that are widely spaced to walk on sand.

Wild pigs

Pigs are hoofed mammals that eat almost anything. They are speedy runners and protective of their little, stripy babies.

The tapir

Tapirs have very long noses and look like pigs, but they belong to a different hoofed family.

Quick, duck!

Tapirs spend much of their time in the water. When threatened they sink under water leaving their nose poking above the surface like a snorkel so they can breathe.

On bended knee

The warthog is a long-legged, African pig. When it feeds it kneels on its wrists.

Malaysian tapir

The nose and upper lip form a trunk.

What is a moose?

Deer of the north
Reindeer live in cold areas in the northern parts of the world. Twice a year they "migrate" – take a long journey – for thousands of miles to avoid bad weather and to breed.

Deer giants
The elk that lives in swampy forests of North America and Europe is the largest deer in the world. Its antlers can grow to 2 m (7 ft) across – bigger than an umbrella – with up to 20 spikes on them.

Deer
Deer are woodland animals that live together in small groups, called herds. They have antlers, which are made of bone.

Deer lose their antlers and grow new ones every year.

Branching out
Only male deer have antlers (apart from female reindeer, who have them as well). Deer antlers are always branched, unlike the pointed horns of cattle.

Moose is the American name for an elk.

The cattle family

The cattle family are hoofed mammals.
They are herbivores, which means they
eat plants. They have four stomachs
to digest the grass they eat.

Early walkers
Like this wildebeest,
many members of the
cattle family are killed
for food by other
animals. Babies are
able to run within
hours of their birth so
they can try to stay
out of danger.

Grazers and browsers
The cattle family all eat
plants. Some are grazers,
who eat low grass. Others,
such as this generuk, are
browsers: they eat from
trees and shrubs.

The herd
Most members
live in large herds for
safety. These bison move
around together according to the
seasons and the food available.

Do members of the cattle family lose their horns yearly like deer?

The horn collection

Unlike deer, members of the cattle family do not have branched horns.

Antelope: these animals have long, pointed horns. Only the males have them.

Bighorn sheep: the horns of the male sheep curve almost in a circle.

Blackbuck: these impressive horns are long and wiggly.

Muskox: their horns curve right down, then up at the tips.

Ibex: this mountain goat has huge, thick horns that curve over its back.

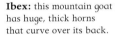
Sitatunga: male sitatungas have long spiral horns.

Wild sheep

Like farmed sheep, wild sheep are good at living in rocky regions.

Barbary sheep

Springing into action

The springbok gets its name from its high spring-like bounces that it does to show predators how fit it is.

Taming the beast

Wild cows, sheep, and goats were tamed thousands of years ago to provide meat, milk, wool, and leather. Modern farm cows are only distant relations of wild cattle.

Jersey cow

Male horses are called stallions and females are called mares.

The horse family

Thousands of years ago, horses were wild animals. Later humans tamed them, and wild horses almost disappeared. Today the only wild horses are zebras and asses.

The hoof

All horses and their relatives have one toe surrounded by a hoof. They run on their tiptoes, which means they can run very fast. All horses have long tails and manes.

Stallion

The hard hoof protects the toe.

Wild horses

The wild horses in the USA are actually tame horses that escaped into the wild hundreds of years ago. They live in herds of one male and lots of females.

How does a horse scratch its back?

Mood swings

Horses communicate with each other by moving their heads, tails, and ears.

Teeth showing: this horse looks quite aggressive but it actually has a happy face!

Ears back: when a horse is angry, it puts its ears back flat against its head.

Ears forward: when a horse is paying attention it has its ears facing forward.

Wild ass

Asses are smaller than horses and have much longer ears. Asses that live with humans are called donkeys. The African wild ass, which is quite rare, lives in the rocky deserts of North Africa.

Stripy horses

Zebras are stripy horses. No-one knows why they are stripy but we do know that, like our fingerprints, each zebra's stripes are unique. They live in Africa in large herds and graze on grass.

Fighting it out

Male zebras fight for females by rearing up or kicking with their back feet. One male will take control of about six females.

Plains zebras

A horse likes to scratch its back by rolling around on the ground.

Hoofed giants

The last members of the hoofed family are by no means the least. They are some of the biggest mammals in the world. Meet the hoofed giants.

Family members
The hoofed giants have cousins, some of which

Okapi: this animal is the only relative of the giraffe. It has a much shorter neck.

Pygmy hippo: this small hippo is a fifth the size of its cousin.

Alpaca: alpacas and llamas are camel cousins that live in South America.

Giraffes
The giraffe is the world's tallest animal. It is taller than three tall men standing on each other's heads!

Healthy appetite
Giraffes are never short of food – they have such long necks that they can reach high leaves on trees.

How much can a camel drink at one time?

The huge rhinoceros

The enormous rhinoceros has skin that is thicker than this book and huge horns that are made of hair.

White rhino

Ships of the desert

Camels live in hot, dry places. Their humps acts like huge food stores of fat that they can use up when there is nothing available to eat.

A one-humped camel is called a dromedary.

The hippopotamus

This mammal giant has a huge, stocky body and stumpy legs. It spends a lot of time in water and it is so heavy it can walk along the bottom of a lake without floating up. A hippo can hold its breath for five minutes.

Indian rhino

Rhinos can run as fast as Olympic sprinters but their speed is no match for a gun. There are very few rhinos left because people kill them for their horns.

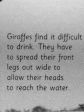

Giraffes find it difficult to drink. They have to spread their front legs out wide to allow their heads to reach the water.

Water mammals

Not all mammals live on land – some live in water. Unlike fish, however, water mammals have to go to the surface to breathe.

Seals

Seals, which include sea lions and walruses, have flippers instead of arms and legs, which make them very good at swimming but not good at walking.

Become an expert..

on the giant mammals of the sea, pages **46-47**

Sea lions can walk more easily than other seals because their flippers are able to move in several directions.

Sea lion

Underwater lives

Seals spend most of their lives in water, but return to land to have babies. They have a thick layer of fat, called blubber, which keeps them warm.

Seals are often very playful in the water.

What noise do seals make?

Otters

Otters are small mammals that have webbed feet to help them swim. The river otter lives along river banks and spends its day swimming to catch food.

Otters of the sea

The sea otter is the smallest sea mammal. It has luxurious, thick fur that keeps it very warm. It rarely comes to land, and even sleeps in the water. When it nods off, it wraps itself up in kelp plants to stop it from drifting away!

Sea cows

Manatees are often called sea cows because they are so big and they "graze", like cows, on river-bed plants. They spend all their lives underwater, and even give birth there.

Walruses

Walruses are huge sea mammals that have massive, blubbery bodies and very wrinkly skin. They heave themselves out of the water to rest and breed.

Walruses use their noses, like pigs, to root around the sea floor for food, such as crabs or sea urchins.

Walrus

In the pink

Walruses are normally greyish-brown in colour. But when they sunbathe, they blush pink because their blood rushes to the surface of their skin to cool them.

Seals bark like dogs!

Ocean giants

Whales and dolphins look like fish but they are actually mammals. They are the biggest water creatures, and some are the biggest creatures on Earth.

Toothed whales

There are two kinds of whales – toothed whales and baleen whales. Toothed whales eat fish and large animals like seals. This killer whale can even leap onto beaches to grab the unfortunate seals.

The big blue

The blue whale is the largest animal in the world – its heart is the size of a small car. It is so big that the next largest creature on Earth, the bull elephant, could sit on its tongue!

Dolphin

Baleen whales

Some whales, such as this humpback whale, have rows of filters called plates, instead of teeth. These are called baleen whales. They gulp huge amounts of water, then sieve it through the plates to remove the food – tiny plants and animals called plankton.

Become an expert...

on water mammals, pages **44-45**
on tiny plankton, pages **140-141**

What animal makes the loudest noise on Earth?

Underwater gossip

Whales live in groups, or pods, and many talk to each other using squeaks, whistles, rumbles, or clicks. Beluga whales "speak" so much that they are sometimes called sea canaries.

Whales

Most whales look quite similar but a few have different features.

Narwhal: this whale has an enormous sword-like tusk, which is actually a tooth.

Porpoise: the porpoise is a toothed whale that looks similar to a dolphin.

Sperm whale: this whale holds the record for the deepest dive of any mammal.

Amazon river dolphin: this dolphin is one of the only freshwater whales.

Leaping dolphins

Dolphins are small whales. They are incredibly intelligent and curious and are often seen leaping alongside boats at sea.

Dolphin

A dolphin's incredibly strong tail helps to lift it high above the surface.

Dolphins leap out of the water to avoid enemies – leaping helps them to swim faster – or to herd fish by making loud splashes.

Spotted dolphin

Underwater babies

Whale and dolphin babies, called calves, grow in their mother's tummys, like other mammals. The calf drinks its mother's milk until it is old enough to eat solid food. Spotted dolphins, like this mother and calf, live in groups of up to 15.

The blue whale is the loudest animal – it makes a very deep rumble.

Birds

Most birds can fly. This has meant that over the years they have been able to live in places that other animals could not get to. They live in every part of the world, even in the chilly Arctic.

Pigeon

Birds are among the most colourful creatures in the world.

Toucan

Finches

Budgerigars

Parrot

Doves

Owl

Hummingbird

Stork

Penguin

Ostrich

Duck

Kiwi

Avocet

Which bird has the most feathers?

Buzzard

Orange-flanked bush robin

Parakeets

Blackbird

Macaw

A world full of birds

There are almost 10,000 different kinds of birds in the world. They range from the enormous, flightless ostrich, which is taller than a man, to the bee hummingbird, which is smaller than your thumb.

Flamingo

Turkey

Chicken

Animal quiz

Take a look through the bird pages and see if you can spot who these body parts belong to.

Become an expert...

on flying mammals, pages **30-31**

on flying insects, pages **110-111**

The world of birds

Only a few animals in the world are able to fly – insects, bats, and birds. But none of them are more powerful or skilled than the bird.

Birds spend much of their time looking after, or preening, their feathers to keep them in good condition.

Feathers are made up of tiny hair-like barbs that all mesh together.

Feathered friends

Birds are the only creatures that have feathers. They use them to fly and to keep warm. Some birds use brightly coloured feathers for display.

A rigid "backbone" or quill runs through the centre of the wing feathers to strengthen them for flying.

Feathers

Different feathers have different jobs on a bird.

Outer wing: strong feathers to provide power in flight.

Inner wing: smooth and flat to help flight.

Tail feather: long and thin for steering and balancing during flight.

Body feather: soft and downy to keep a bird warm. Some have exotic colours.

Become an expert...

on nest-making, pages 54-55
on exotic birds, pages 72-73

What is the world's smallest bird?

Flight

A bird can fly because it has wings and a very light skeleton – many of the bones are hollow. Birds have short and compact bodies that make them neat fliers too.

There are two methods of flying; flapping, like this red-tailed minla, and gliding.

Red-tailed minla

By flapping its wings up and down, the bird remains in the air.

Travelling birds

About one-third of birds spend summer in one place then when the winter sets in they fly thousands of miles to a warmer spot. Often they go to exactly the same places year after year.

Feet

The shape of birds' feet vary depending on where they live.

 Eagle foot: birds of prey have sharp talons to kill and grip animals.

Perching foot: songbirds have three toes in front and one behind for perching.

Webbed foot: waterfowl have webbed feet to help them to paddle on water.

Ostrich foot: two thick toes help this flightless bird to run very fast.

Bills

The shape and size of a bird's bill, or beak, can show what they eat.

 **Duck:** wide and flat to tear plants and filter food underwater.

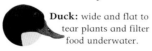 **Woodpecker:** long and hard to chisel into wood and pick out insects.

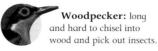 **Chaffinch:** short and cone-shaped, ideal for cracking seeds.

 **Heron:** long, ideal to stab fish underwater.

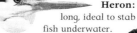

Communication

All birds have good hearing so they can respond to songs from other members of their family. Birds are well known for their tunes, and some, like this parrot, even speak.

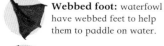

Courtship

At various stages in her life, a female bird will be on the lookout for a mate. Males go out of their way to impress the ladies, often in spectacular ways.

Fierce competition

There is often competition between the males to attract the females so performances have to be very slick. This female has chosen her mate.

Crowned cranes

A good decorator

The male satin bowerbird builds an avenue of twigs, and at each end he places a collection of anything he finds attractive, such as shells, bones, or berries. The female picks the nest she finds the most appealing.

weird or what?
Some birds of prey perform amazing aerobatic displays. The male and female lock talons in mid-air and fall almost to the ground before swooping up again.

In which season do birds start courting?

Pairing off

It is important for birds to find the right partner.

Peacock: the male shows off by shaking his spectacular tail.

Swans: when a male and female swan mate, they stay together for life.

Pheasant: male pheasants fight aggressively with each other for females.

Building a home

The male weaver bird builds an incredible nest that hangs from a branch. When a female passes he hangs beneath it fluttering his golden wings and shrieking to her to join him.

Spotted-backed weaver

Foot dance

The blue-footed booby has blue feet, which are attractive to the females. When he wants a mate he dances and lifts his feet to show them off.

Once cranes have selected a partner they dance together, then bow, leap, bounce, and make sudden frantic runs.

Show off

The male frigate bird has a huge, red neck pouch, which he inflates with air when he is looking for a mate. When a female passes he wobbles it around and makes gobbling noises to impress her.

Among true cranes, seven of the fifteen species are in danger of extinction.

Nesting

All birds lay eggs, which other animals find tasty. To keep their eggs safe, many birds build nests.

A city in a nest
Some weavers, called social weavers, build one huge nest to hold lots of birds. This only happens in dry regions, however, if they got too heavy with rain they would fall.

Hummingbirds are the smallest birds in the world.

Weaver bird

Out of reach
The most important thing about a nest is that no enemies can reach it. For this reason many birds build their nest in trees.

Weaver birds goes one step further than building nests in trees; they build them hanging down from branches.

Tiny home
This hummingbird has built its nest on a fir-cone. Some hummingbirds use spiders' webs to secure their nests.

Which birds are able to tie knots?

When a bird has made its nest, it turns around and around in it until it has made a perfect hollow.

Nests

Some birds go to great lengths to make amazing-looking nests.

Tunnel home: some weaver birds build nests with tunnel entrances.

In the reeds: the reed warbler builds his nest between thin reeds.

Mud nest: the domed ovenbird makes its nest entirely out of mud.

Tree trunk: A blue tit has built this nest in a hollow tree trunk.

Ground eggs

Some birds don't make nests at all. Instead they lay their eggs on the ground. These Eurasian oystercatchers' eggs are camouflaged against the pebbles.

The eggs are speckled and can barely be seen.

A perfect fit

Round, hollow nests like this are called cup nests. Birds build them in trees using twigs, feathers, moss, and anything else they can find.

Pileated woodpecker

Handy holes

Hollowed-out trees are good places to keep eggs safe. Woodpeckers make nests by chiseling through the wood with their sharp beaks. The following year birds, such as parrots, may use it.

Safety in numbers

Along the west coast of Africa, thousands of cape gannets lay their eggs at the same time, right next to each other. This reduces the chances of the eggs being eaten.

Eggs

Birds' eggs have a hard shell. Predators can crack them quite easily so they must be kept safe.

Southern cassowary egg

Hatching out

Making or finding a nest is a lot of work for birds, but looking after the eggs and chicks is even harder!

Inside the eggs each chick grows using the yolk as food.

Blue tit family

Nest birds

The mother bird sits on her nest keeping the eggs warm until they hatch. When they are born they need constant feeding until they can look after themselves.

At one day old the bald chicks are very hungry.

At three days old the chicks are demanding constant food. Their bright mouths are easily seen by parents.

After two weeks there is barely enough room to move. The chicks are now ready to fly away.

At nine days their feathers are starting to appear and the nest is getting crowded.

Baby birds

There are two types of young bird. Nest birds are born blind and naked and depend completely on their parents. The other type, like ducklings, hatch with open eyes and a coat of downy feathers.

Duckling

Waterbirds

Waterbirds are often born on the ground rather than in nests, so they have to be able to get out of danger quickly. Ducklings take to water very soon after hatching.

The chick has an egg tooth that it uses to poke through the shell.

It then pushes against both ends and breaks itself out of the egg.

Egg tooth

Which bird builds the biggest nests in the world?

Swan family

A female swan lays up to eight eggs
in a clutch and only she looks after them.
When the chicks are born both parents
take care of them for about five months.

These swan chicks catch a ride
on their mother's back.

Wren

Feeding frenzy

Both parents help to feed
their chicks. They can
make up to 1,000 trips
a day between them to
bring back enough food.

Rotten parents

Cuckoos don't look after
their chicks. Instead the
female lays her egg in
another bird's nest. When
it hatches, the
chick kicks out
the other eggs.

The cuckoo
chick is fed
by the adopted
parents, and
is often bigger
than they are.

The bald eagle.

Songbirds

Most of the world's birds are part of a huge family known as the songbirds. They spend a lot of their time in flight.

A variety of birds

The songbird family are all very different in looks, habits, and songs.

Robin: European robins are easy to spot because of their red tummies.

Blackbird: the blackbird often sings in the evenings from a high perch.

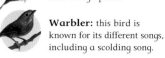
Warbler: this bird is known for its different songs, including a scolding song.

Special feet are useful for perching on very thin twigs.

The short beak is used to break hard surfaces, such as nutshells.

Songbirds can sleep on twigs and branches without falling off.

Blue tit

Foot perch

Songbirds, or perchers, all have a unique type of foot that means they can grip onto even the thinnest branches. Three of their toes point forwards and one points backwards.

Finding food

Like this song thrush, most songbirds are small, but they use up a lot of energy flying so they need a lot of food. They feed on small insects, worms, and snails.

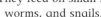

Where in the world   can only birds survive?

Young chicks learn their songs by listening to the adults.

Bird songs

Each species of songbird has its own special song, using different notes and rhythms. Males tend to sing more than females.

Songbird parents feed their chicks until they are 10-15 days old.

Dawn chorus

Dawn in Europe and North America is when male songbirds sing loudly to attract females. Somehow the females seem to hear the correct tune in the noise!

Safety in flocks

Many songbirds live in groups, called flocks. They collect food together and join forces to fight off bigger birds that might eat them.

weird or what?

The Australian lyrebird can not only imitate other birds' songs but also other sounds it hears in the rainforest, such as chainsaws and even camera clicks!

Songbirds, are small and compact in shape, with tiny beaks.

Dunnock

Birds are the only vertebrates that can survive in Antarctica.

59

Life in the air

Some birds are spectacular acrobats. They are the experts of the air – one or two can even fly backwards! Many of these birds spend most of their lives in the air.

Hummingbirds

These tiny birds beat their wings in a figure-of-eight pattern. This means that they can hover and fly backwards! Smaller species beat their wings 80 times a second.

Hummingbirds have long beaks that can poke into flowers to sip the nectar.

Magenta-throated woodstar hummingbird

Air acrobats

Swifts, swallows, and martins have forked tails that help them to control their flight. They can catch insects while they are flying and even, like this swallow, swoop down over water and drink without landing.

Record holder

The smallest bird in the world is the bee hummingbird. Found in Cuba, it feeds on nectar from flowers. Its eggs are smaller than peas!

Bee hummingbird

There are some flying insects that are bigger than this bird.

Swallow

60

What is unusual about the sword-billed hummingbird?

Nesting

Swifts, such as this chimney swift, spend a lot of their time in the air but they must land when they are ready to nest.

Swallows' nests

Swallows collect mud pellets and mould them into cup-shaped nests. These can often be seen beneath the eaves of buildings. The parents feed the chicks by hovering near them rather than landing.

Swallows have small beaks, but big mouths to catch insects in mid-air.

Forked tail

Become an expert...

on other nesting methods, pages 54-55

Nesting in burrows

Sand martins look similar to swallows. They make their nests by digging burrows in soft earth along riverbanks or by cliffs.

The swift

Swifts can spend a lot of time in the air without landing. They can catch insects and even sleep on the wing!

Swift

It is the only bird whose beak is longer than its body.

61

Freshwater birds

If you search around fresh water anywhere in the world you will find teams of birds living on it or near it. Some are swimmers and others are waders.

The male mallard makes a lower pitched quack than the female and whistles as well.

Swan

Geese

Mallard duck (female)

Mallard drake (male)

Kingfishers

Kingfishers live by rivers. They perch on branches above the water waiting for fish to swim past. When they see one, they dive!

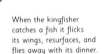

When the kingfisher catches a fish it flicks its wings, resurfaces, and flies away with its dinner.

Waterfowl

Ducks, geese, and swans are waterfowl. They have boat-shaped bodies and webbed feet, which make them very good swimmers.

Bottoms up!

Waterfowl have long bills with sharp ridges along them to grip slippery fish. Mallards often feed by sticking their bottoms into the air to reach plants.

What are baby swans called?

Flamingo

This stork, with its hunchback and bald neck, is often described as ugly.

Black-crowned night heron

Wattled jacana

Marabou stork

Heron

Waders

Waders have long legs that allow them to walk in shallow water without getting their feathers wet. Some also have long necks for finding food.

Have a stab

Herons are found living next to rivers and lakes. They eat fish, which they catch by darting their S-shaped neck forward at lightning speed and stabbing the fish with their sharp beak.

Pink flamingos

Flamingos live in huge flocks, of sometimes a million birds! Many of them are pink because they eat tiny shrimps that dye their feathers pink.

Flamingos sleep in the water, often on one leg.

Flamingos' bills act like sieves to filter out tiny food from the water.

Flamingo

> **Become an expert...**
> on migrating birds, pages **76-77**
> on sea birds, pages **64-65**

Baby swans are called cygnets.

Sea birds

Many birds spend
their lives next
to the sea or out
on the open ocean.
Some only return to
land to breed and
raise young.

A life at sea

A lot of sea birds, such as this
albatross, have webbed
feet that help them swim,
and special beaks to hold
slippery fish.

The albatross has the largest wingspan of any bird

Webbed feet

Dramatic divers

The sea is full of food and birds have
various ways to catch it. Some chase fish
underwater while others, such as gannets
and boobys, dive down like torpedoes
from the air to snatch them.

Other sea birds

The coastlines of the
world are always
packed with sea birds.

Herring gull: this
bird is common in Europe
and North America.

Inca tern: this bright
bird lives on the west
coast of South America.

Cormorant: this bird
can also be found inland
in Europe, Asia, and Africa.

Pelican

Pelicans
also use their
large mouth to
catch rainwater
for drinking.

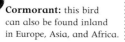

A mouthful of fish

The pelican dives underwater
and scoops up fish in its large
mouth. It can fit three times
more fish in its mouth pouch
than in its stomach!

How long can birds survive without returning to land?

Cliff birds

These black-legged kittiwakes, like many other birds, live in huge, noisy groups on cliff faces. They even nest and lay their eggs on the narrow ledges.

Kittiwakes

The cliffs are a safe place to rest, away from enemies.

The albatross' beak is hooked, with special ridges to help it hold onto fish.

A flock of gulls

Gulls can often be seen in huge numbers along the sea shore. They eat almost anything, raiding rubbish dumps and stealing other birds' eggs.

Puffins

The puffin has webbed feet and small wings, which it uses like fins to swim, as well as to fly. It raises its one chick, called a puffling, in a burrow.

The puffin can dive to depths of 60 m (200 ft).

Puffin

Become an expert...

on the ultimate sea bird – the penguin, pages **66-67**

What a lot of fish!

Atlantic puffins have large, colourful beaks. The top bill and tongue are ridged with spikes that enable it to hold lots of fish at one time.

Some do not return to land for five years!

In the chill

You have to be pretty tough to survive the freezing temperatures of the Antarctic. But some birds not only survive but thrive in the chill.

Penguins cannot fly but they sometimes leap into the water from icebergs.

The penguin

Most penguins, such as these emperor penguins, live in colonies, which can consist of hundreds of thousands of birds.

Water wings

Penguins may look clumsy on land and can't even make it into the air, but in the water they are are master swimmers. They use their wings as flippers and their tail and feet to steer.

Keeping warm

To keep them warm in the snow and icy water, penguins have a dense covering of waterproof feathers and many layers of fat.

Egg

How long can a penguin stay underwater?

Other snow birds

One of the few birds that lives and breeds on Antarctica all year round is the snow petrel. It is completely white, which keeps it hidden in the snow.

Penguins' feet are positioned so far back that when they stand upright, they have to use their tail to balance or they would topple over backwards.

Adult penguins have white tummies and dark backs, which help to camouflage them in the water.

Penguin predators

Antarctic skua

This Antarctic skua lives on or near the ice in Antarctica and nests at the coast. It eats penguin eggs and even baby penguins if they are left unguarded.

Penguin parents

King penguins tuck their egg under their bellies resting it on their feet. The parents take turns to look after it. When king penguin chicks are born they are covered in brown, downy feathers.

Become an expert...

on flightless birds, pages **78-79**

on other sea birds, pages **64-65**

In very cold conditions chicks and penguins huddle together for warmth.

Slip-sliding around

Penguins find it hard to walk, so they often slide on their belly over snow and ice, pushing with their flippers and feet.

The chicks must be fed until they grow adult, waterproof feathers

Birds of prey

With their huge wings, sharp talons, and hooked beaks, birds of prey are the hunting kings of the bird world.

African hawk eagle

Hunting

Many birds of prey spot an animal on the ground from very high up in the air with their excellent eyesight. They swoop down and grab it with their sharp talons.

Birds of prey are the only birds that kill with their feet.

Secretary bird

These birds are famous for eating snakes, which they kill by stamping on them.

Walkabout

Secretary birds have incredibly longs legs. They rarely fly, instead they can be seen taking long strides across the grasslands of Africa.

The eagle is the most powerful of the birds of prey, it can kill an animal as big as itself.

Which is the fastest bird of prey?

The vulture

Vultures are the waste collectors of the world, eating dead animals before they rot. They very rarely kill their own food.

Red tailed buzzard

Buzzard's wings are huge, which means they are fast flyers and can glide and even hover without flapping their wings.

Vultures

Vultures are very clean birds. After eating they will often fly long distances to have a bath.

A vulture's taste

Vultures don't just eat dead animals. This Egyptian vulture, enjoys eggs as well.

The Egyptian vulture loves ostrich eggs but cannot break them with its beak. Instead it uses a stone to crack the egg.

Ostrich egg

The osprey

Ospreys have such good eyesight that they can spot fish swimming underwater. They swoop down to the surface and scoop the fish up in their sharp talons without landing on the water.

The peregrine falcon – it can dive down towards its prey at 270 kph (168 mph).

Night flyers

As the sun sets most birds settle down for a good night's sleep. Owls and nightjars, however, are preparing for a night of hunting.

Nightjars spend most of their waking life in the air. Their legs and feet are rarely used.

Owl types

Owls come in all sizes and colours and can be found around the world.

Great horned owl: this regal-looking owl has ear tufts or "horns".

Spectacled owl: this owl lives in the South American rainforest.

Snowy owl: this owl has extra feathers on its feet, to keep it warm, like slippers.

Burrowing owl: the burrowing owl makes its nest underground.

Nightjars

Nightjars rest on the ground during the day. At night they hunt, plucking insects out of the air as they fly.

Hidden from sight

During the day owls sleep, often in branches of trees. Their feathers camouflage them so well, as on these scops owls, that people very rarely notice them.

Barn Owl

Hooked beaks help to tear up food.

Owls

All owls, such as this barn owl, hunt in darkness and must rely on their amazing eyesight and hearing to help them.

Owls have sharp talons to grip and tear apart animals that they eat.

Many owls have velvety fringes around their flight feathers that make their wings very quiet as they fly through the air.

Owl eggs are almost completely round.

What is the smallest owl in the world?

Hunting by night

All owls eat small animals. They swoop silently on their victims in the dark and grab them in their sharp talons.

Tawny owl

Most owl chicks learn to fly when they are two months old. In the meantime their parents feed them.

In the dark owls sometimes find animals only by the sounds they make.

Owls like to eat small animals, such as mice, and small birds.

Eating

Owls cannot chew so they swallow their food whole. When they have digested the animal they cough up the bones and fur as a small pellet.

If you tear one of these pellets apart, you can see the whole skeleton of the animal it has just eaten.

An owl's mouth may look quite small but it can open very wide indeed.

Owl pellets

Iranian eagle owl chicks

Owl chicks

Rather than build nests, owls prefer to lay their eggs in holes of some kind – in trees or buildings. The male and female both help to feed the chicks.

The elf owl – it is only 15 cm (6 in) tall.

Exotic flyers

Tropical rainforests and places with warm climates are filled with exotic and colourful birds, which are often very large.

The toucan uses its massive bill to reach for fruits on the tips of branches.

Although the bill looks heavy, it is hollow so is very light.

Toucan

This species of toucan lives in the top of the rainforest canopy.

Chestnut-eared aracari

Toucans have two toes facing forwards and two facing backwards.

Toucans
These birds live in the South American rainforest and surrounding areas. They are famous for their huge bills.

Birds of paradise
These exotic birds are from Papua New Guinea. This raggiana bird of paradise is showing off his beautiful feathers to a female by opening his wings and shaking them at her.

Where do budgerigars live in the wild?

These birds fly together in large flocks.

The parrot family

Parrots are very colourful and often very noisy. They are strong fliers and good climbers. Parrots include macaws, budgerigars, lovebirds, and parakeets.

Crested cockatoos

These parrots, called cockatoos, have a bright yellow crest on their head, which they raise when they are frightened or angry.

Rainbow lorikeet

Scarlet macaw

Nuts about nuts

Almost all parrots eat plants, such as fruit, nuts, and seeds. They are the only birds that hold food up to their mouths using their feet.

These lorikeets are the most colourful of all parrots. They can be found along the east coast of Australia.

Budgerigars are popular as pets for their ability to mimic sounds and "talk".

Become an expert...

on the exotic, colourful creatures of the ocean, pages **144-151**

They live in Australia.

Gamebirds

Gamebirds live most of their lives on the ground. Most are plump with a small head, short wings, and sturdy, strong legs.

Some gamebirds, like these chickens, are raised specifically to provide food for humans.

Hen

Cockerel

Good-looking males

Like most male gamebirds, this cockeral is more brightly coloured than the hen. They use their fine feathers to attract females.

Sport

Gamebirds, such as this male common pheasant, are hunted by humans for sport, which is why they are called gamebirds.

This male common pheasant has a tough, hooked beak for digging up plant roots and insects to eat.

Males have brightly coloured feathers

The tail drags along the ground behind the male when not spread out.

Gamebirds are champion egg layers, producing more than 20 in one nest — more than most other birds.

Nesting

Most gamebirds nest in shallow holes in the ground. This is the reason the females are duller in colour — so that they are camouflaged against the ground when they are nesting.

Some gamebirds don't sit on their eggs, instead burying them underground to keep them warm.

Where are wild turkeys commonly found?

The peahen chooses her peacock as her mate based entirely on his looks.

The peacock lifts his tail and shakes it at the female.

Peacock

Peahen

An amazing tail

The male peacock has the most spectacular tail in the animal world. When he wants to attract attention he raises it high.

to attract females

Vertical take-off

Gamebirds are strong runners and prefer to run away from danger rather than fly. When very afraid, however, they are capable of rocketing upwards quickly with frantic, flapping wing beats.

Reeve's pheasant

When they fly upwards at speed, their wings make a whirring sound that can startle enemies.

This ptarmigan is half way through its autumn to winter change.

Colour change

Not all males have bright feathers. Both male and female willow ptarmigans change their colours throughout the seasons so they are always camouflaged.

Gamebird chicks escape danger on the ground because they are able to run and fly soon after hatching.

Become an expert...

on other courtship displays between birds, pages 52-53

Pheasant chicks

Globetrotters

The great advantage birds have is that they can fly. This means they can choose the warmest part of the world to live in at any one time.

Record holder

The Arctic tern is the biggest traveller of all. Each year it flies the whole way around the world from the Arctic to the Antarctic and back again.

Arctic tern

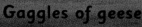

Arctic
Greenland
EUROPE
Canada
NORTH AMERICA
ATLANTIC OCEAN
AFRICA
PACIFIC OCEAN
CENTRAL AMERICA
SOUTH AMERICA
To Antarctica

Migration

Many birds have a summer and a winter home in different places. Their journey from one place to another is called migration.

Travelling birds

Birds have different travel habits. Some fly non-stop, some rest on the way.

Song thrush: small birds are night fliers and use the stars to find their way.

Buzzard: birds of prey wait for a warm day and glide for long distances.

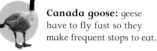

Sanderling: waders carry a lot of food so they can fly non-stop.

Canada goose: geese have to fly fast so they make frequent stops to eat.

Swan: these birds fly by day or night and rest if visibility gets poor.

Ruby-throated hummingbird: this bird crosses the Gulf of Mexico to get to South America.

Gaggles of geese

Each winter tens of thousands of snow geese leave Canada for a 2,000 km (1,250 mile) trip to California and Mexico. They follow exactly the same route each year.

What proportion of the world's birds migrate each year?

Become an expert...

on waterfowl,
page **62-63**

on birds of prey,
page **68-69**

Birds of prey

Hawks, buzzards, and eagles
from North America fly
south to warmer climates
as the winter
approaches.

Bald
eagle

Eagles use warm air currents
to help them glide

Knots

Knots leave the Arctic in the
autumn and fly towards South
America. They travel over the
2,000 miles of ocean non-stop.

"V" formation

Many birds fly in a "V"
formation because the bird
in front makes the air easier
to fly through for the
ones behind.

About one-third of all birds in the world migrate.

Flightless birds

Some birds cannot fly even though they have wings. Often, as a result of this, they become excellent at running or swimming instead.

New Zealand birds

There are so few mammals here that some birds have no need to fly.

Kakapo: this ancient, flightless bird is the world's rarest parrot.

Kiwi: the kiwi lives on the ground. Its feathers are so small they look like fur.

Takahe: these birds are almost extinct. There are only 40 pairs left.

The ostrich has a long neck and a small head.

Rapid runners

Ostriches are the fastest bird runners in the world. In fact they are faster than racehorses – they can reach speeds of 75 kmh (45mph).

Ostrich

The ostrich is the only bird in the world to have only two toes.

The ostrich

Ostriches are the world's largest birds. They have feathers to keep them warm, which look more like fur. Even though they can't fly they still have small wings, which are useless.

Moving in flocks

Like flying birds, ostriches and emus like to live in large groups called flocks.

Which bird lays the largest eggs?

2 1

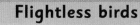

Flightless wings

One reason birds have wings is to make a quick escape from predators - animals that want to eat them. If birds don't have predators, they have no need to fly and may lose this ability over time.

Flightless birds, like this rhea, have tiny useless wings that they don't use.

Penguins

The penguin uses its wings as flippers to "fly" underwater. Its feathers are short and stiff to help keep them warm in cold climates.

Flightless cormorants

The Galapagos islands off western South America have no mammals that kill birds, so their cormorants have lost the ability to fly. They have become good swimmers.

Become an expert...

on penguins, pages **66-67**

on bird's eggs, pages **56-57**

Rearing rheas

Most birds' eggs are looked after by their mothers, but in the rhea family the father is in charge. He sometimes looks after up to 60 eggs, all from different mothers, in one nest.

Large flightless birds have thick legs, which help them to run fast.

Rheas and emus have three large toes that all face forward.

Dad looks after the babies until they are five months old.

The ostrich.

79

Reptiles and amphibians

Flying gecko

Caiman

Reptiles and amphibians are the "cold-blooded" creatures of our world. Most amphibians, which include frogs and toads, live near water. Reptiles, such as snakes and lizards, are found both on land and in water.

Anole lizards

Green tree python

Spectacled caiman

Common snake-necked turtle

Common snapping turtle

Madagascan day gecko

Rattlesnake

Cold blooded

Cold-blooded creatures do not have cold blood. Cold blooded means they are the same temperature as the air or water around them. If they are cold they sunbathe, if hot they seek shade.

Are snakes reptiles or amphibians?

Reptiles have scaly skins.

Green Anaconda

Ornate horned toad

Indian starred tortoise

European common frog

Diadem snake

White's tree frog

Asian tree toad

Green iguana

Animal quiz

Take a look through the reptiles and amphibians pages and see if you can spot who these skins belong to.

Become an expert...

on other creatures with scales in the fish section, pages 142-151

81

Snakes are reptiles.

The world of reptiles

Reptiles are egg-laying animals that have a tough skin covered in scales. They live on land and in water.

The reptile groups

There are four main groups of reptiles:

The tortoise family: these reptiles all have a shell over their bodies.

Snakes and lizards: the majority of reptiles fall into this group.

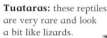

The crocodile family: this group are the giants of the reptile world.

Tuataras: these reptiles are very rare and look a bit like lizards.

Reptiles can eat huge meals, then go without food for days.

Most reptiles, like this lizard, swing their bodies from side to side when walking.

Eating habits

Reptiles are meat eaters, with the exception of tortoises, which move too slowly to catch fast-moving prey. Lizards, such as this gecko can eat half their own weight in insects in one night.

All reptiles shed their skin from time to time.

Flying gecko

Hot and cold

Reptiles have scales, which can control how much water they lose through their skin. This means they can live in dry places. They are cold blooded, however, so rely on the climate to keep their temperature in check.

European eyed lizard

Reptile babies

Nearly all reptiles lay eggs, which hatch into miniature versions of their parents. A few such as this slow worm, however, give birth to live young.

This lizard, which lives in the desert basks on rocks to warm up its body

What is the longest snake in the world?

Tuataras live in burrows and hunt at night. They can live for 100 years.

Living fossils

Tuataras are the only survivors of a group of reptiles that lived with the dinosaurs millions of years ago. Today they live on a group of islands off New Zealand.

Scaly skin

A reptile's skin is covered with scales made of keratin, like your nails.

Tortoise: the shell of a tortoise has lots of large, hard scales on it.

Lizard: Lizards' scales have stretchy skin between them.

Crocodile: these scales are strengthened in between by bony plates.

Snake: the skin on snakes has overlapping scales for extra protection.

Reptile relatives

The reptiles of today are the last living relatives of dinosaurs and look very similar to their ancient ancestors. You can see similarities between the *Tyrannosaurus rex* and this lizard.

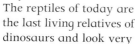

Tyrannosaurus rex

Become an expert...

on other creatures that have shells – snails, pages **132-133**

Collared lizard

Under a shell

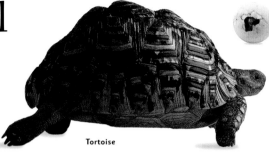
Tortoise

You can spot tortoises or turtles because they carry their homes on their backs – these domes, called shells, are attached to their bodies.

Shell shapes

Shells are hard so protect the body. They come in many shapes.

Turtles

Starred tortoise: high domed shells are difficult to attack.

African red-necked turtle: flatter shells help turtles slip through water.

Red-footed tortoise: these tortoises have unusually long shells.

Tortoise or turtle?

The main difference between these two reptiles is that tortoises live on land and turtles live in water.

The Galapagos tortoise can live to 150 years old.

Tortoises

Tortoises walk very slowly because of their heavy shells. They have short, stocky legs that support their weight. They mainly eat plants and eat nearly all day.

Turtles

Turtles live under water. They sometimes poke their heads out to breathe, but they can also breathe through their skin. Some can stay under the surface for weeks.

Do tortoises have teeth?

Eggs and babies

Most turtle and tortoise shells are completely round, like ping-pong balls. Some are hard, but others are quite soft to touch. The babies peck their way out of the eggs.

Tortoises and turtles are born complete with their shells.

Hinge-back tortoise

Hiding on the spot

When a tortoise feels threatened it quickly pulls its legs and head under its shell, and keeps very still. The shell is too hard for any animal to eat.

Tortoises' shells are made of bone

Experts believe that tortoises lived among the dinosaurs 200 million years ago and have changed little since.

Race to the ocean

Turtles return to land to lay eggs – sometimes thousands of them on one beach. When they hatch, the babies all make a rush for the sea where they will live.

Galapagos giants

The biggest tortoises in the world live on the Galapagos Islands off the coast of South America. They can be 1.8 m (6 ft) long – that's as long as a man is tall!

Tortoises sometimes eat insects, but they are not usually fast enough to catch them.

No, instead they have razor-sharp jaws that can snip twigs and leaves.

Introducing lizards

There are over 40,000 different types of lizard living in every habitat from deserts to rainforests. They are particularly fond of hot places.

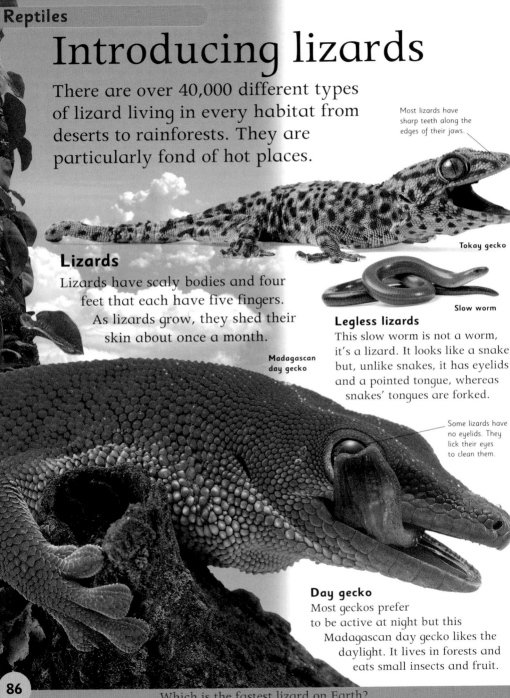

Most lizards have sharp teeth along the edges of their jaws.

Tokay gecko

Lizards

Lizards have scaly bodies and four feet that each have five fingers. As lizards grow, they shed their skin about once a month.

Slow worm

Legless lizards

This slow worm is not a worm, it's a lizard. It looks like a snake but, unlike snakes, it has eyelids and a pointed tongue, whereas snakes' tongues are forked.

Madagascan day gecko

Some lizards have no eyelids. They lick their eyes to clean them.

Day gecko

Most geckos prefer to be active at night but this Madagascan day gecko likes the daylight. It lives in forests and eats small insects and fruit.

Which is the fastest lizard on Earth?

Flying lizards
Lizards can't fly but some can glide from tree to tree. This lizard has skin around its body that opens out, like a parachute.

Getting around
Lizards are extremely agile. They can run very fast, some climb trees, some can even walk on water!

Climbing lizards, such as this chameleon have long claws that grip onto branches.

Eggs
Most lizards lay eggs on the ground.

Laying: lizards lay their eggs among leaves on the ground or in sandy holes.

Eggs: the eggs are soft and leathery – easier to break out of.

Hatching: after two to three weeks the lizards hatch.

Babies: the baby lizards look like their parents.

Chameleon

The chameleon's tail helps it to balance when it perches on thin twigs.

Sticky fingers
Geckos have special toe pads covered in millions of tiny hair-like spikes. These spikes can grip any surface, so geckos are able climb up walls and even along ceilings.

Walking on water
When they want to go faster some lizards, like this crested water dragon, run on their hind legs. The basilisk lizard above can even run for short distances across the surface of the water, its wide feet pushing it along at high speed.

Crested water dragon

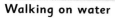

The racerunner can run at 29 kph (18 mph) – that's faster than most people can run.

87

Hunting and defence

Lizards are incredibly fast runners, so they can get away from danger quickly. They also use their speed to catch smaller animals for food.

Get lost!
When the frilled lizard feels threatened it doesn't run away. Instead it opens its umbrella-like frill around its neck, rocks its body and hisses loudly. This is often enough to scare the enemy away.

normally folded flat – when it opens

The frilled lizard also lashes its tail backwards and forwards.

The loose skin on the frilled lizard is

Become an expert...
on insect defence, pages 114-115
on fish defence, pages 148-149

Frilled lizard

What is unusual about a chameleon's eyes?

Hunting and defence

Chameleon

Lunch time
Lizards are meat eaters. Some eat small animals; some can eat animals bigger than themselves. This chameleon flicks out its enormous, sticky tongue and catches insects on the tip.

Losing the tail
Some lizards are able to detach part of their tail if it is grabbed. Often the tail will carry on wiggling when it has broken off, which can distract the enemy.

This tree skink has broken its tail and is growing a new one.

out, the lizard looks four times bigger

The Komodo dragon can grow to 3 m (10 ft) long.

Enter the dragon
The Komodo dragon is the largest of all lizards. It is so powerful it can catch and kill animals bigger than itself. It has a long forked tongue that it uses to taste the air and search out dead animals. It lives in Indonesia.

A touch of poison
The Gila monster is one of only two poisonous lizards. When it has caught a victim, it chews the poison into them to kill them.

Thorny devil

Gila monster

Thorny defence
The thorny devil has the ultimate defence. It has sharp spines all over its back, which makes picking it up and eating it very difficult indeed.

Chameleons can move their eyes in different directions.

89

Slithering snakes

Snakes can survive anywhere, from cold climates to the hot deserts and rainforests of the world – you can even find them underwater.

Getting around

Snakes have no arms and no legs. Instead they have a bendy body that wriggles. Some slither in a straight line, others like this viper wiggle in an "s" shape.

A snake's forked tongue flicks in the air to smell food or alert it to enemies.

Red-tailed racer

Types of snake

Snakes can be divided into four different groups, or families.

Typical snakes: this family is the biggest of the four.

Vipers: they have poisonous fangs and live in the hot places.

Constrictors: kill their prey by squeezing them to death.

Poisonous snakes: they are some of the most deadly creatures alive.

Snakes have no eyelids, so they cannot blink.

Snake senses

Snakes can't see or hear very well but they can smell much better than you or me. They use their forked tongues to smell and taste the air around them.

Become an expert ...

on snake defence, pages 92-93
on the snake-like eel, page 149

What is the smallest   snake?

Some tree snakes have ridges on their bellies, which help them to grip onto branches.

Tree climbers
Many snakes live in trees, coiling themselves around the branches. They tend to have long tails to help them climb and balance.

Snakes have very bendy bodies

Tree snakes can find birds' nests in the trees using smell in order to attack and eat the chicks.

Snakes everywhere
Snake body shapes are sometimes adapted to where they live. Ground snakes have heavy bodies to slide through soil, while sea snakes have oar-like tails for swimming.

Most sea snakes, such as this sea krait are incredibly poisonous.

Hibernating
Snakes can't control their body temperature very well so those that live in cold climates often have a long sleep, or hibernation, during the winter. They can survive for many months without eating.

Garter snakes

Laying eggs
Snakes lay eggs but most do not make good parents. The python coils itself around its eggs to keep them warm, but most snakes leave them so the young must fend for themselves.

Attack and defence

All snakes eat animals, including smaller snakes. But other animals also find snakes a tasty meal so they have to be experts at defending themselves as well as hunting for food.

Forms of defence

Snakes have many other defences that protect them from enemies.

Playing dead: the grass snake lies with its mouth open pretending to be dead.

Camouflage: this viper's colouring camouflages it among the leaves.

Rattlers: the rattle snake shakes its tail making a loud, frightening noise.

Protection

Snakes have various ways to protect themselves. Some snakes, such as this forest pit viper, have long fangs, containing deadly poison, or venom. When threatened they bite.

When danger threatens, the cobra rears up its head and hisses. If this doesn't frighten the enemy away, it strikes.

Spitting cobra

Attack

Cobras are among the most dangerous snakes on Earth; their poison can easily kill humans. This spitting cobra squirts poison at its victims, which can permanently blind them.

Which is the most poisonous snake in the world?

Cunning

Snakes creep up on their victims then lunge at them incredibly quickly. They kill larger victims before they eat them either by poisoning or crushing them.

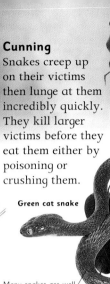

Green cat snake

Many snakes are well camouflaged against their background, which makes it easier for them to stalk victims.

Eating habits

Snakes eat pretty much anything that moves, from ants and snails to goats and crocodiles. The egg-eating snake can swallow eggs bigger than its head! It then squeezes the insides out and vomits up the shell.

Egg-eating snake

The snake's jaws are elastic and stretch wide to allow it to eat big animals.

The egg is squashed by muscles inside the snake's body.

A tight squeeze

Constrictors, like this anaconda wrap themselves around their victims and squeeze them until they can't breathe. This snake will eat this large alligator whole!

Snakes can eat so much in one meal that they don't have to feed for weeks.

Become an expert...

on how lizards defend themselves against enemies, pages 88–89

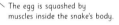

93

The "fierce snake", found in Australia, is the most poisonous.

Crocodiles and alligators

Lurking beneath the water are the monsters of the reptile world. Meet the wild, ferocious crocodilian family.

Crocodilians

There are three types of crocodilians; gharials, alligators, and crocodiles.

This animal is a caiman, a type of alligator that lives in Central and South America.

The family

Crocodilians are large, meat-eating reptiles that live in water, but sometimes hunt on land as well. They all have very powerful shutting jaws.

Crocodilians have three eyelids on each eye – one acts like goggles underwater.

Gharial: this crocodilian has a long thin snout.

Alligator: it has a shorter, broader snout and lives in the Americas.

Crocodile: unlike the alligator, it has teeth showing when its mouth is closed.

Although crocodilians have

Water beasts

Crocodiles and alligators live in water and are very good swimmers. Their eyes and nostrils are on top of their head so that they can see, breathe, and hunt with the rest of their bodies underwater.

Spectacled caiman

Most crocodilians live in freshwater rivers and lakes, although a few species also venture out to sea.

Day to day

Crocodilians lead fairly lazy lives. During the morning and evening they lie on banks basking in the sun with their mouths open. This helps them to warm up or cool down. They spend the night in the water.

How big can crocodiles grow?

Parenting

The crocodilian family make very good parents. Males attract females by bellowing and blowing bubbles. The female lays her eggs near the water and guards them fiercely.

The temperature at which the female keeps the eggs determines whether they are male or female.

Nile crocodile

Parenthood

The female stays with the eggs until they hatch into tiny versions of their parents. Often the mother will then pop the babies into her mouth and carry them to the safety of the water.

many teeth, they cannot chew. They shake and tear meat

Become an expert...

on other reptiles that enjoy the water – turtles, **pages 84-85**

Crocodiles and alligators only have about 50 meals a year.

A large appetite

Crocodilians are some of the world's great meateaters. Often, like this crocodile, they wait at the water's edge for an animal to take a drink, then they attack, grabbing it with their massive jaws. They can kill animals bigger than themselves.

Crocodiles can grow to a massive 6 m (20 ft) – that's as long as a large car.

The world of amphibians

Amphibians are different from reptiles in that they have smooth skin with no scales. They are born in water then live on land or in water when they grow up.

Fire salamander

Amphibian family

There are three groups in the amphibian family.

Frogs and toads: these amphibians have no tail and big back legs.

Newts and salamanders: these lizard-shaped animals live on land or in water.

Caecilians: these worm-like creatures have no legs.

Amazing skin

Most adult amphibians, such as this salamander, can breathe through their skin as well as their lungs. In order for the skin to breathe it has to be kept moist, which is why most amphibians like to live near water.

Frog

Some frogs live in water...

Become an expert...

on mammals that also like to live in water,

pages **44-45**

Colourful creatures

Many amphibians are incredibly colourful creatures. Some are spotted, others are striped and some are just very bright.

What is the world's most poisonous frog?

A choice of home

Frogs and toads can live both on land and in water. Some even live in trees.

Land frogs tend to be more rounded in shape than water frogs.

Water living

Some salamanders spend the whole of their lives underwater. This cave salamander does not have any lungs; it breathes through its skin only. It is almost completely blind.

...other frogs prefer to live in the tops of tall trees!

Caecilians

Legless caecilians are rarely seen by humans because they live either under water or under ground. They have a pointed head, which they use as a shovel.

If an animal is poisonous it is often a very bright colour that warns predators.

Travelling parents

Each spring salamanders, newts, frogs, and toads lay their eggs in ponds or streams. Some travel 5 km (3 miles) to get there.

Common newt

97

The most poisonous frog is the bright-yellow poison-dart frog.

Frogs and toads

Frogs and toads have short, tubby bodies and large heads with bulging eyes. They have no visible neck and most have a very wide mouth. Frogs and toads live in lots of different habitats around the world.

Frogs often have longer back legs than toads.

White's tree frog

Frog or toad?

There are not many differences between frogs and toads. Toads tend to have warty skin, while frogs have smooth skin.

In order to leap, the frog straightens its legs and pushes away

North American leopard frog

Frogs leap to move around and to escape danger.

Legs and leaping

Frogs are well known for their high leaps into the air, which they make using their muscular back legs. Because these are longer than the front ones, they stay folded until it's time to jump!

Making more frogs

Each spring thousands of frogs return to the water to find a mate and lay their eggs. Large clumps of these eggs, called spawn, are laid together, covered in jelly to protect them.

Tadpoles live under water until they are frogs.

Spawn

How many eggs can frogs and toads lay in a lifetime?

Toads' feet are less webbed than frogs'.

Oriental fire-bellied toad

Time for a chat

Frogs and toads are true talkers. They croak to attract females and alarm enemies. This toad has an inflatable vocal sac – a big piece of stretchy skin that helps make an extra-loud sound.

Running frogs

Not all frogs leap to move around. These African running frogs live in grassy areas where they prefer to remain low. So they raise their body off the ground and run.

The African running frog is in the crouching position.

To move, it raises itself up and takes long strides forwards.

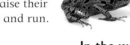

Webbed feet

from the ground

Frogs often dive into water for safety.

In the water

Frogs and toads are very good swimmers. They have webbed feet, which help them move quickly through the water. They swim by bending their legs in and out, just like people do in the breast stroke.

Junior frogs

Frog and toad eggs hatch into tadpoles, which are completely different from adults. They look like tiny fish with no legs and a long tail. Over four months the tadpoles gradually grow legs, lose their tail, and turn into miniature frogs.

Most frogs and toads abandon their eggs, so the tadpoles must look after themselves.

When a frog is fully formed, it can leave the water.

Tadpoles have gills to breathe with, a bit like fish. They develop lungs when they become frogs.

Hunting and hiding

Frogs and toads eat small animals. But they also make an ideal meal for others because they have no fur, feathers, or claws. They have clever ways to avoid becoming food.

This four-eyed frog has fake eyes on its bottom to make it look like a big animal.

Finding a meal

Frog and toad adults are meat eaters. They have very wide mouths so they can eat quite big animals.

This toad sits and waits for animals to simply walk past it. It then opens its mouth and swallows them whole.

Ornate horned toad

Defence

Frogs and toads have many defences: some use poison, some use camouflage, and others can almost fly!

Handle with care

Some frogs, like this poison dart frog, are highly poisonous and taste disgusting when eaten. They tend to be very brightly coloured – nature's way of warning enemies off.

A sticky end

Frogs and toads have sticky tongues that grab onto prey. They can shoot these out, grab the insect or small mammal, and swallow it whole! Both creatures have to blink when they swallow –their eyeballs help to push the food down the throat.

European common frog

How does the European   common toad defend itself?

ree frogs have
huge sticky
pads on their
eet that help
hem to grip
into trees.

They can change direction in the air

Leaping to safety

Some tree frogs are masters
of the air. This Wallace's
tree frog has webbed feet.
When it feels threatened, it
leaps into the air, spreads
its toes, and uses them as a
parachute to glide from
branch to branch.

**Wallace's
tree frog**

**Asian
horned
toad**

Spot the toad

The Asian horned
toad has one of
the best defences.
It simply becomes invisible, using
camouflage. Its body is flat, like a leaf,
and exactly the same colour. Even the
flaps over its eyes are leaf-shaped.

**Become
an expert...**

on the way insects
defend themselves
from their enemies,
pages **114-115**

101

It stands on tiptoe and blows itself up with air, like a balloon.

Salamanders and newts

These animals may look like lizards, but they have far more in common with frogs and toads. They have smooth skin and they love the water.

They have long, slender bodies and long tails.

Most newts and salamanders live in cool, damp forests.

Newts and salamanders must keep their skin damp in order to breathe.

Newt or salamander?

Newts and salamanders are very similar animals, but newts live on land and breed in water, while salamanders spend their whole lives in the water.

This newt lives under rocks or in caves to keep its skin moist.

How big is the biggest salamander?

Getting around
These creatures normally move slowly but they can move quickly when in danger. They crawl over land and at the bottom of ponds. Newts sometimes swim at the surface of the water.

This North American tiger salamander can grow to 40 cm (15 in).

Eating habits
Salamanders and newts are insect eaters who like to eat fresh prey. They find their food using smell and sight. Salamanders have long tongues that flick out to catch prey.

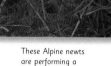

This Mandarin salamander is eating an earthworm.

Colourful displays
Many newts and salamanders are brightly coloured. The male sometimes shows off his colours to females when looking for a mate.

Egg laying
Eggs are laid in the water, and when they hatch out they look very like frog tadpoles. Unlike frogs, however, they keep their tails when they grow up and gain legs. They live in the water until adulthood.

Great crested newt

Half formed
Mexican axolotls are salamanders that have never quite changed fully into adults, but have remained half formed. They live underwater and are sometimes kept as a pets.

These Alpine newts are performing a courtship dance.

Creepy crawlies

Black housefly

Cave spider

Lacewing

In this book, the world of creepy crawlies consists of all the animals that don't belong to the other sections. All creepy crawlies are invertebrates.

Spiderwasp

Common housefly

Speckled bush cricket

Red giraffe weevil

Hornet

Flea

Tachinid fly

Caterpillar

Cardinal beetle

Dragonfly

Locust

Land snail

Spiny-bellied orb weaver spider

104

What family do snails belong to?

Blue morpho

Golden emperor

Large yellow underwing

Queen Alexandra's birdwing

Spineless creatures

Invertebrates include all the different insects, plus other small land animals, such as spiders and snails, and extraordinary-looking sea creatures.

Cuttlefish

Squid

The sea creepy crawlies include octopuses, starfish, and even coral.

Krill

Starfish

Common octopus

Animal quiz

Take a look through the creepy-crawly pages and see if you can spot where these pictures come from.

Become an expert...

on sea mammals, pages **44-47**

on sea birds, pages **64-65**

The world of insects

A huge majority of creepy crawlies are insects. In fact there are more types of insect in the world than any other animal. They are absolutely everywhere. Some are almost too small to see and others are surprisingly large.

Remember, insects have 3 + 3. Three pairs of legs and three body parts.

Most insects have two pairs of wings.

Beetle

What is an insect?
You can tell if a creepy crawly is an insect because insects always have six legs. They also have three body parts – a head, a thorax, and an abdomen.

When a pile of dung appears in Africa, dung beetles are on the scene in minutes.

The beetles roll perfect balls of dung in which they lay a single egg. When the egg hatches it eats the dung.

Nature's recycling service

Although many people dislike insects and they can be pests, they are also essential to our world. In fact we could not live without them. For instance, these dung beetles do a very good job cleaning up dung.

Dung beetles

Apart from honey, what else does a bee produce that we can use?

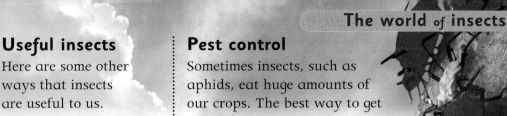

Useful insects

Here are some other ways that insects are useful to us.

Red food dye: this food colouring is made from the bodies of scale insects.

Silk: believe it or not, the silk you wear is made by silk-moth caterpillars!

Honey: if there were no bees in the world, we would have no honey.

Food: to some people, such as the Australian aborigines, grubs are a meal.

Pest control

Sometimes insects, such as aphids, eat huge amounts of our crops. The best way to get rid of them is to introduce another insect that likes to eat them. Ladybirds are often used for aphid pest control.

Aphid

Introducing insects that eat other insects is called biological pest control.

Ladybird

Aphids breed so quickly that it is difficult to control them.

As old as an insect

We know that insects were around 40 million years ago because some were trapped in a tree resin called amber, which hardened back then and preserved them.

Become an expert...

on beetles, pages **120-121**

on bees, pages **122-123**

and their poison is used as medicine.

Bees produce wax

Egg to adult

The one thing insects are very very good at is making more insects. They all start off as eggs, then grow up in lots of strange and different ways.

Metamorphosis

When they're born, many insects look nothing like their parents. They have to go through three stages – egg, larva, and pupa – before they become adults. This process is called metamorphosis.

Dragonflies have to shed their outer skin in order to grow.

Every insect in the world lays eggs

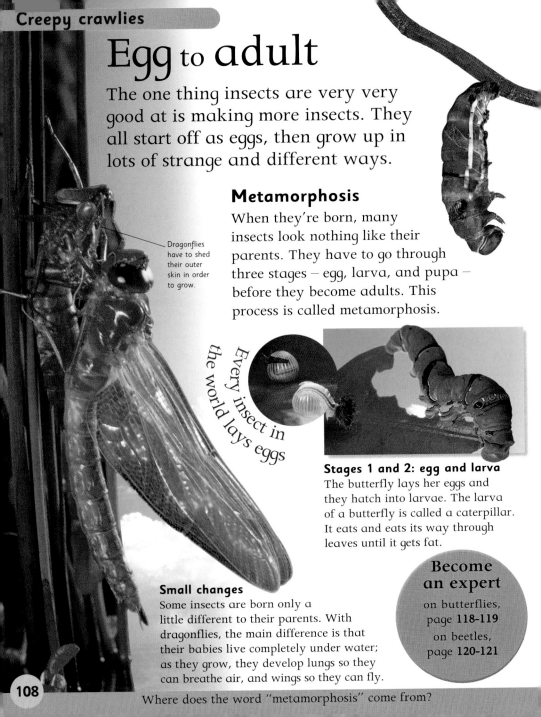

Stages 1 and 2: egg and larva
The butterfly lays her eggs and they hatch into larvae. The larva of a butterfly is called a caterpillar. It eats and eats its way through leaves until it gets fat.

Small changes
Some insects are born only a little different to their parents. With dragonflies, the main difference is that their babies live completely under water; as they grow, they develop lungs so they can breathe air, and wings so they can fly.

Become an expert
on butterflies, page **118-119**
on beetles, page **120-121**

Where does the word "metamorphosis" come from?

The caterpillar has to find a safe place to make its pupa – pupate.

Stage 3: pupa
When the caterpillar is big enough, it sheds its skin, fastens itself to a plant stem and creates a pupa – a hard shell – around itself.

Stage 4: adult
Inside the pupa an amazing change takes place. Eventually it splits open and the adult butterfly emerges.

When it's ready, the butterfly pumps fluid around its body to help split the shell.

The butterfly must wait for its wings to flatten out and dry before it can fly away.

A pupa can remain like this for weeks or even months.

Ladybirds
Like butterflies, ladybirds go through metamorphosis.

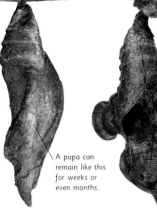

Eggs: the female lays a group of eggs on a leaf.

Larva: the eggs hatch out into larvae, called nymphs.

Pupa: a month after hatching, each larva builds itself a pupa.

Young ladybird: A week later, a yellow adult emerges.

Adult: After a while the yellow colour turns to red with black spots.

The butterfly stretches out its crumpled wings.

White admiral butterfly

Parental care
Most insects abandon their eggs after they have laid them. These shield bugs, look after their babies very protectively, but this is rare.

Metamorphosis is Greek for "change of body form and appearance".

On the move

Insects are very good at getting from "a" to "b". Some run, others fly, some jump, and a few even swim!

Flying

All flying insects have two pairs of wings but they use them in different ways. Beetles fly with one pair and the second, harder pair fold over the top to protect them.

In order to fly, the beetle spreads its wing cases, opens out the delicate wings, and jumps into the air.

Cardinal beetle

The flying wings are very fragile so the beetle needs hard cases to protect them.

Other wings

Here are some more ways insects use their wings. Many are very good air acrobats.

Common fly: flies only use one pair of wings. The other pair look like sticks.

Dragonfly: it uses both pairs but can operate each side separately.

Lacewing: this insect can use four wings separately and can fly backwards.

Hoverfly: the hoverfly beats its wings so fast you can barely see them.

This water boatman hangs upside down beneath the surface.

Water boatman

Diving beetle

Swimming

Some insects spend much of their time under water, using their legs like paddles. Diving beetles have special hairs on their legs that splay out in the water and help them swim.

Caterpillars can loop up steep twigs

Looping caterpillar

Which insect can run the fastest?

Locust

Darkling beetles can run at 1 m (3 ft) per second.

Darkling beetle

A tiny flea can jump 100 times its own length. It can also jump 600 times per hour non-stop for three days while looking for an animal to settle on.

Jumping

Some insects can jump huge distances by using their back legs as powerful springs. If a grasshopper is disturbed its catapult-like legs help it to get away.

Running

Insects' legs reflect where they live. Beetles that live under bark have short legs that don't get in the way. Darkling beetles have long legs that let them race across hot sand in the desert.

Become an expert...

on caterpillars,
pages **108-109**

on flies,
pages **126-127**

Locusts can jump up to a metre (3 ft) high.

These caterpillars have suckers at either end of their bodies to hold on to, and loop up, twigs.

Flea

The green tiger beetle.

Eating habits

Insects eat a wide range of foods. Some are meat eaters and some are vegetarians, but most spend their waking life eating. Insects have mouthparts for either biting and chewing or piercing and sucking.

This hummingbird moth has a long tongue to suck nectar with. It feeds while it is flying.

Meat eaters

Many insects eat other insects and have to find cunning ways to catch their meals. This praying mantis hides among leaves then strikes.

The praying mantis can sit still for a long time waiting for its meal to walk past.

Vegetarians

Most insects are vegetarians and munch or sip constantly during their lives. Some like to bite and chew food like leaves, others suck liquid, such as flower nectar, through their tongues.

Antlion larva is sometimes called a "doodlebug".

Meaty meals

The antlion larva buries itself under ground with its open mouth facing the sky and simply waits. When an ant runs over the hole, it falls straight into the antlion's jaws and is eaten swiftly.

How do hawker dragonflies catch insects?

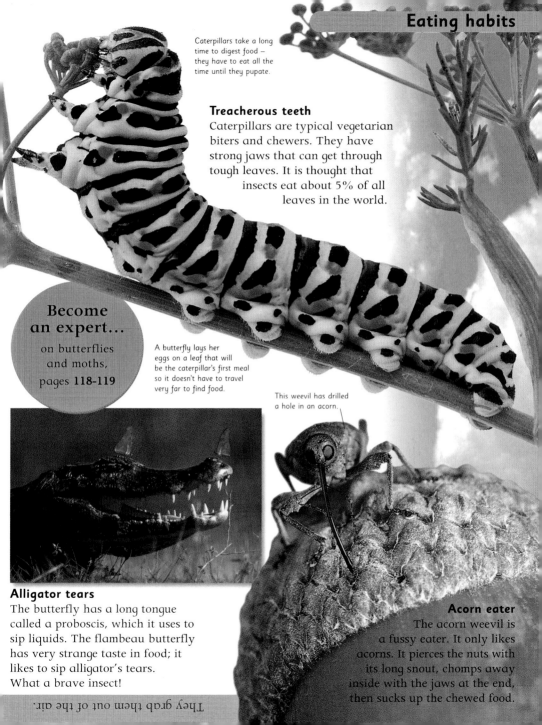

Caterpillars take a long time to digest food — they have to eat all the time until they pupate.

Treacherous teeth

Caterpillars are typical vegetarian biters and chewers. They have strong jaws that can get through tough leaves. It is thought that insects eat about 5% of all leaves in the world.

Become an expert...

on butterflies and moths, pages 118-119

A butterfly lays her eggs on a leaf that will be the caterpillar's first meal so it doesn't have to travel very far to find food.

This weevil has drilled a hole in an acorn.

Alligator tears

The butterfly has a long tongue called a proboscis, which it uses to sip liquids. The flambeau butterfly has very strange taste in food; it likes to sip alligator's tears. What a brave insect!

Acorn eater

The acorn weevil is a fussy eater. It only likes acorns. It pierces the nuts with its long snout, chomps away inside with the jaws at the end, then sucks up the chewed food.

They grab them out of the air.

Defence

Many insects make delicious meals for other animals. So it is very important indeed that they have some defence against the enemy.

Camouflage

Orchid mantis

A good way for insects to "disappear" is to hide amongst plants. This white orchid mantis is hiding in plants that are the same colour as it is. Can you see it?

The orchid mantis can change colour from pink to white depending what colour flower it is on.

Become an expert...

on how fish defend themselves, page **148-149**

Lost among leaves

This katydid, a kind of bush cricket, looks so much like a leaf that it even has veins on its back. All it has to do is keep very still.

The butterfly's "eye"

Which insects look exactly like brown twigs?

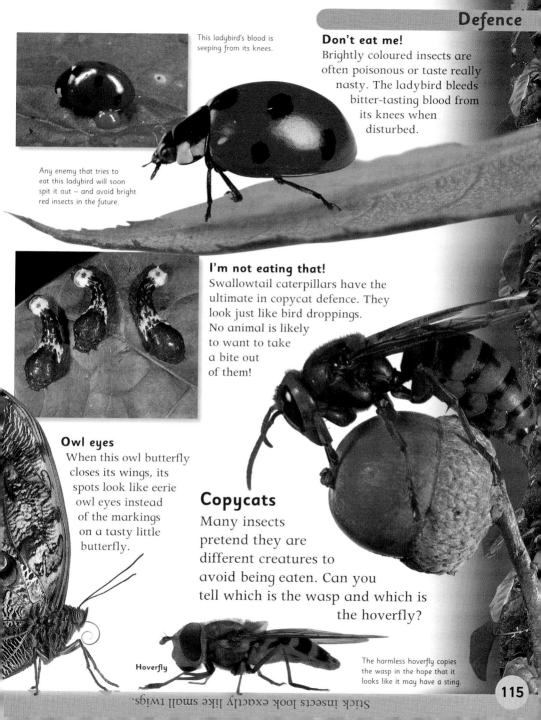

This ladybird's blood is seeping from its knees.

Don't eat me!
Brightly coloured insects are often poisonous or taste really nasty. The ladybird bleeds bitter-tasting blood from its knees when disturbed.

Any enemy that tries to eat this ladybird will soon spit it out – and avoid bright red insects in the future.

I'm not eating that!
Swallowtail caterpillars have the ultimate in copycat defence. They look just like bird droppings. No animal is likely to want to take a bite out of them!

Owl eyes
When this owl butterfly closes its wings, its spots look like eerie owl eyes instead of the markings on a tasty little butterfly.

Copycats
Many insects pretend they are different creatures to avoid being eaten. Can you tell which is the wasp and which is the hoverfly?

Hoverfly

The harmless hoverfly copies the wasp in the hope that it looks like it may have a sting.

Stick insects look exactly like small twigs.

Pests and plagues

Insects are small but they can do a huge amount of damage. It may be hard to believe but these are some of the most dangerous creatures alive.

Some more pests...

Humans have a hard time controlling pests. For thousands of years, we have been trying to find ways to get rid of them.

Colorado beetle: this little beetle can destroy whole potato fields.

Common clothes moth: these moths love to eat woollen clothes.

Longhorned beetle: these beetles can destroy entire forests of trees.

Unwanted guests

Cockroaches have tough bodies and are very difficult to kill.

Once cockroaches move into your home they are very difficult to get rid of. They eat rotten food and spread diseases around the house. They also make a house smell.

Cockroach

Become an expert...

on tiny animals that live on your body and can make you ill, pages **140-141**

Head lice

The head louse is a tiny insect that grips onto your hair so tightly that it is tricky to remove. It drinks blood from your head and makes your scalp itchy. Its eggs are called nits.

Close-up of a headlouse's claws

What are bedbugs?

Tsetse fly

Hungry locusts

When the rains fall in Africa, millions of locusts sometimes gather together and move in huge groups, or swarms. They eat everything in sight and there are so many of them that they blot out the sunlight.

Bloodsuckers

The tsetse fly is a blood sucker. It pierces the skin of humans and other animals and sucks their blood. Here you can see the fly with an empty and a full tummy. It spreads a disease called sleeping sickness.

Only female mosquitoes drink your blood.

If a mosquito sucks blood from a sick person, it will pass the illness on to the next person it bites.

Male mosquitoes drink nectar from flowers, and juices from plants.

Mosquito

Keep away!

Believe it or not, the mosquito has killed more people on Earth than any other animal. When it bites it spreads a dangerous disease called malaria.

Malaria kills thousands of people every year.

Bedbugs are tiny insects that suck your blood when you sleep.

Butterflies and moths

Butterflies and moths are unique insects because their wings are covered in tiny scales. They look alike but there are a few slight differences.

Brown brindled beauty moth

Arctiid moth

Hartig's brahmaea Moth

Which is which?

Butterflies have club-shaped antennae, or feelers, and moths tend to have feathery or plain antennae. Butterflies are also generally more colourful than moths.

There are now no silk moths left in the wild – they are all bred to make silk.

Purple emperor butterfly

Red glider butterfly

Monarch butterfly

Madagascan moon moth

This moon moth has no mouth as it only lives long enough to lay eggs, and doesn't have time to eat before it dies.

Resting

Butterflies come out by day and moths emerge at night. When moths rest they open their wings, while butterflies rest with their wings closed.

Eighty-eight butterfly

Banana eater butterfly

Scaly skins

Both butterflies and moths have tiny scales on their bodies and wings that overlap like tiles on a roof.

This Millar's tiger moth has its wings open.

This peacock butterfly has its wings closed.

Which is the biggest butterfly in the world?

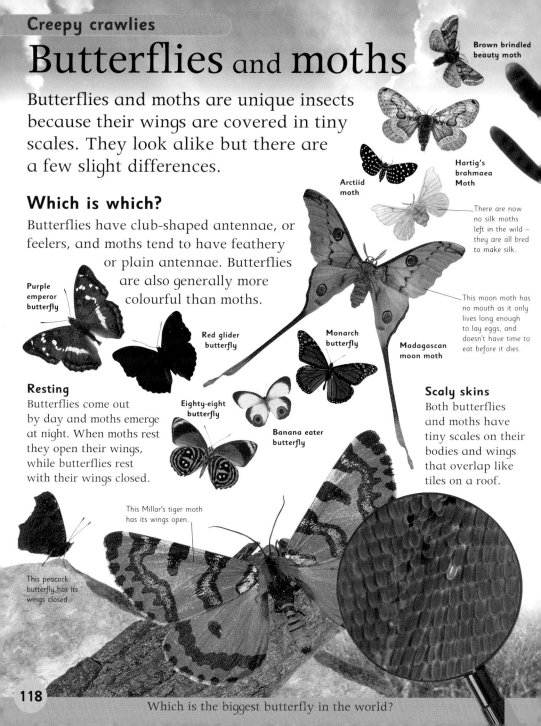

Incredible migration

The monarchs are unusual butterflies. When the cold winter sets in they undertake an incredible journey. They travel from Canada to the fine weather in California, USA, and Mexico and can cover 130 km (80 miles) in a day.

Trees are often covered in monarch butterflies as they rest.

Caterpillars spend most of their time eating.

Antennae are used for smelling

Tasty titbits

Caterpillars make very tasty snacks for many other animals, so they have various cunning ways of stopping things from eating them.

 Puss moth caterpillar: it rears its colourful head when threatened.

 Swallowtail caterpillar: it disguises itself as a bird dropping.

 Postman caterpillar: it is covered in long spines.

Eating

Butterflies and moths hatch as caterpillars, which eat in a completely different way to the adults.

Butterflies keep their tongues rolled into a coil until they want to eat. They then unroll it and use it like a straw.

Hungry caterpillar

Caterpillars have strong jaws, which they use to chew leaves with. When they become butterflies their mouthparts are different – instead they have a long tongue, or proboscis, which they use to sip liquid.

Tongue, or proboscis

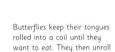

Become an expert...

on how caterpillars change into butterflies, pages **108–109**

Beetles and bugs

These tiny creatures can be found all over the world, from mountain tops to scorching deserts. You can never escape beetles and bugs.

African Goliath beetle

Beetles

Beetles are the most heavily armoured of all insects. They have biting and chewing mouthparts.

The African Goliath beetle is the biggest beetle in the world.

The diving beetle uses its legs as paddles.

Diving beetles

Most beetles live on land, but the diving beetle catches its food – tadpoles and even small fish – in the water. In order to breathe it tucks a bubble of air under its wings before every dive.

Beetles

Beetles are often bright and beautiful colours.

Scarab: this beautiful golden scarab is found in South America.

Chafer beetle: these lovely beetles vary hugely in size and colour.

Weevil: this bright blue weevil is found in Papua New Guinea.

Frog beetle: frog beetles can be bright red and very shiny.

How do most bugs taste their food?

Glow in the dark

Glowworms are not worms, they are beetles. They have a special organ in their bodies that lights up in the dark. They flash their bodies at night to talk to each other.

Glowworms can sometimes be seen at night glowing and flashing in their thousands.

Glowworms are found all over the world.

Bugs

Members of the bug family look quite like beetles, but they have a feeding tube that pierces and sucks up their food. They cannot bite and chew.

Clicking cicadas

Cicadas, a type of bug, are the noisiest of insects. They can be heard up to 1.5 km (1 mile) away. They make their noise by vibrating drum-like pads on the side of their tummies.

Bugs

They are small, but some can be quite aggressive!

 Shield bug: it is known as the "stink bug" because it can let out a foul smell.

 Coreid bug: this bug waves the flags on its legs to scare predators.

 Aphid: this little creature is a pest. It attacks garden plants.

 Assassin bug: it kills other insects and sucks their insides out.

weird or what?
The deathwatch beetle eats through wood. When it wants to attract another beetle's attention, it bangs its head against the wood. Sometimes people hear the tapping in their houses.

Some cicada species can live for up to 17 years!

Most bugs taste their food through their feet.

Bees and wasps

You may think bees and wasps simply buzz a lot and sting, but they are actually some of the most intelligent insects around.

Bumble-bees do not produce large amounts of honey.

Class system

Bee societies have three classes within their colony.

Queen: each bee colony has a queen who lays up to 100 eggs a day.

Drone: there are only ever a few drones – males – with the queen.

Worker: all of the workers are female. They collect the nectar.

The bee has special baskets on its legs to collect pollen in.

Bees

Bumble-bees and honey-bees live in large colonies, working together as a group. Worker bees spend much of their lives gathering nectar from plants, which they turn into honey.

Worker bees cannot lay eggs. Only the queen provides new babies.

The honey is their food.

weird or what?

When a honey-bee knows that a flower is full of nectar, it does a special waggling dance to show other worker bees where to go to collect it.

Comb

A honey-bee's home is a miniature city made of wax, produced by the bees, in cell shapes. This is called a honeycomb. Some cells hold the baby larva and some hold honey.

True or false: bees die immediately after they sting.

Wasps

Wasps either live alone (solitary wasps) or in large groups (social wasps). Those that live together build large nests made out of dead wood that they chew into paper.

Common wasp

Bees and wasps have powerful biting mouthparts.

Wasps

There are many different families of wasps. Most adults have a narrow waist between their second and third segments, and large eyes.

The queen begins building the nest, then when her first babies are big enough, they take over.

The wasps chew and chew dead wood until it becomes pulpy, it then dries into paper.

Stings

Wasps and bees have yellow and black stripes that warn people they are poisonous. They only sting when they feel threatened or they are defending their home.

Sting

Living alone

Many wasps do not live in groups, but prefer to live alone. They are called solitary wasps. They are mostly parasitic, laying their eggs on other insects.

Ichneumon wasp (solitary)

Moving in swarms

When a new queen is born, she will leave with a group of wasps to build and rule her own nest. The wasps all fly off together in a group called a swarm. In this picture they are resting.

Ants and termites

There are more termites and ants on Earth than any other insect species – there are millions of them. They live in groups called colonies.

Ant

Termites

Termites live in tropical, or hot, areas. Each colony has a queen who is the chief and she has a king. Workers clean and feed, and soldiers guard.

Ants

There are many different types of ant, one or more living in every corner of the world. These are leaf-cutter ants, which collect leaves and turn them into food.

Queen

Termite soldiers

The fierce termite soldiers have big jaws to bite anything that disturbs their queen or their home.

In some species the queen grows into a huge egg-laying machine producing 30,000 eggs in a day!

Termite mounds

Some termites live in huge mounds, which they build using earth, saliva, and their droppings – one piece on top of another, like bricks. Some mounds can be up to 7 m (25 ft) high.

The walls of termite mounds are so hard that you would need a pick axe to get into them!

Inside the mound

Inside the mound there is a network of rooms and passages. At the centre lies the nursery containing the queen and her eggs.

Which ants live in colonies of up to 300,000 individuals?

Working together

Some ants and aphids – a type of bug – are very good at keeping each other happy. The aphids give off a sweet liquid that the ants like to sip, so in return the ants guard the aphids and protect their eggs for them.

Aphids eat a lot of tree sap, so ants and aphids often live on trees together.

Become an expert...

on aphids and other bugs, pages **120-121**

There are 8,000 different kinds of ant in the world.

Living larder

Honeypot ants live in the desert. The workers fill chosen ants with nectar, which they turn to honey and store in their big tummies. When food is short they vomit it up and feed the colony with it. The honeypots are too big to move.

Wood ants live in these enormous colonies.

Flies

There's no escaping them; flies are all over the place. Lots of people hate them because many spread diseases and a lot of them bite. But flies have their uses and we couldn't live without them.

Disease carriers

Flies like rotting food and as they have sticky feet, they can carry bacteria from one piece of food to another, which can carry nasty diseases.

Housefly

A fly uses special spongy mouthparts to suck up food.

A fly vomits on food to turn it to liquid, and then it sucks it up

Maggots

Fly babies

Flies often lay their eggs, which hatch into maggots, in manure or rubbish. Unlike adults, maggots do not have wings and they chew their rotten meat rather than suck it up. They eventually turn into pupas, then flies, just like caterpillars turn into butterflies or moths.

Flight

Flies are very good flyers, which is why they are difficult to swat. This hoverfly can beat its wings up to 1,000 times per second! Sometimes it changes direction so quickly that it seems to disappear.

Become an expert...

on other pests, pages **116–117**

pages **108–109**

Where do mosquitoes lay their eggs?

Housefly

Sticky feet

The housefly has sticky feet that allow it to walk up walls and across ceilings. It rubs its feet together to get dust and dirt off, which helps keep them sticky.

A fly's uses

If there were no flies in the world, there would be a lot more rotting food and dead animals around. Although we may think they are nasty, they actually do a very good job eating rubbish.

Flies lay their eggs on rotten food. When the eggs hatch they eat it up.

Fly collection

There are many species of fly and they come in all shapes and colours.

Tachinid fly: these flies are small, bristly, and often brilliantly coloured.

Crane fly: this fly is better known as the daddy-long-legs.

Robber fly: this fly has extraordinary, feathery back legs.

Bee fly: these little flies look like bees and are quite stout and very hairy.

We know that flies can see very well with their big eyes, but no-one really knows if they see the world very differently to us.

Bluebottle

Flies have fine hairs on their legs that can sense tiny movements.

Mosquitoes lay their eggs in still water, which is why they often live near ponds.

The world of non-insects

There are many creepy crawlies scuttling around our planet that are not insects. Some live on land, others live in fresh water or the sea. They come in all sorts of weird and wonderful shapes.

Arachnids

Spiders, scorpions, ticks, and mites belong to a land-dwelling family called arachnids. All arachnids have eight legs and two body parts.

Tarantula

The worm family

Segmented worms like earthworms are simple animals that have a head at one end, a tail at the other, and lots of segmented body parts in between. They live on land or in water.

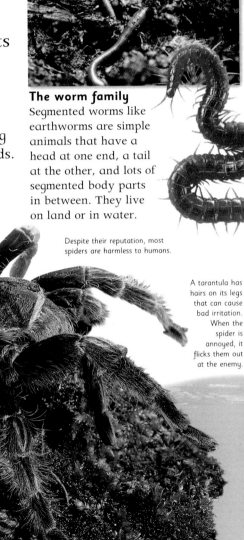

Despite their reputation, most spiders are harmless to humans.

A tarantula has hairs on its legs that can cause bad irritation. When the spider is annoyed, it flicks them out at the enemy.

Become an expert...
on spiders and scorpions, pages 130-131

128

Odd sea creatures

The sea contains some very strange animals indeed. Here are a few:

Sponge: these animals were once thought to be plants.

Starfish: most starfish have five arms to crawl across the sea floor.

Anemone: these flower-like sea animals have no brains.

Molluscs

Slugs, snails, squids, and oysters, are molluscs. Some live on land and some live in water.

Snail

Snails are found on land and in the sea.

The octopus, which is also a mollusc, is a very intelligent creature.

Centipede

Centipede

Centipede

Millipede

Centipedes have one pair of legs on each segment and millipedes have two pairs on each.

Centipedes and millipedes

If you try counting the legs on an insect and you find there are too many, the chances are you have found a centipede or millipede. They have lots and lots of legs.

Crustaceans

Most crustaceans, such as lobsters, crabs, and shrimps, live in water. Only the woodlouse lives on land. They often have a shell and their eyes are on stalks.

Lobster

Some spiders can grow as big as dinner plates!

Spiders and scorpions

Spiders and scorpions are the best-known members of the arachnid family. They are two of the most feared creatures on Earth, despite the fact that most are perfectly harmless to humans.

Spiders

There are about 40,000 species of spider in the world. They can all bite but most are not dangerous to humans.

Of all spiders, jumpers have the best eyesight.

Jumping spider

This is the silk line that the jumping spider attaches to something before it jumps.

The jumping spider spots a fly and leaps, attached to a line of silk,

Ticks are so small that you can barely see them.

Scorpions

Scorpions live in warm climates and feed on insects. They hold their prey with their big pincers and paralyse it with the sting at the end of their tail, which they bend right over their back.

This jungle scorpion is carrying her babies on her back until they can look after themselves.

Sting

Bloodsucking ticks

A tick is also an arachnid. When it feeds, it attaches itself to an animal and bites the flesh. When it has drunk enough blood it drops off.

Some scorpions grow to lengths of 15 cm (6 in).

Scorpion

How many pairs of eyes do spiders have?

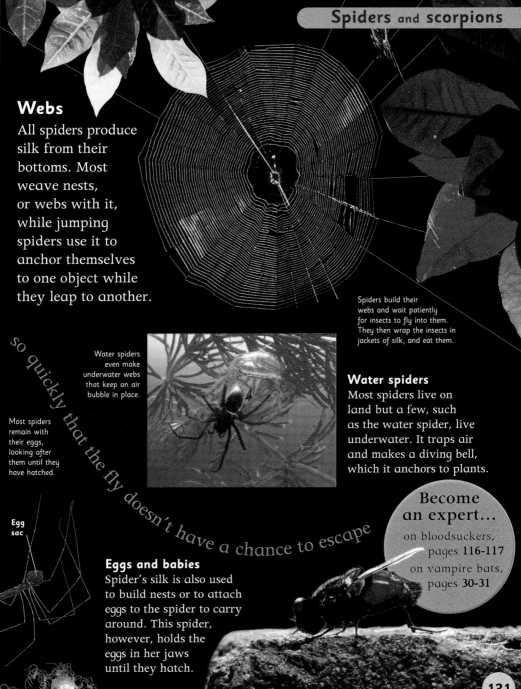

Webs

All spiders produce silk from their bottoms. Most weave nests, or webs with it, while jumping spiders use it to anchor themselves to one object while they leap to another.

Spiders build their webs and wait patiently for insects to fly into them. They then wrap the insects in jackets of silk, and eat them.

Water spiders even make underwater webs that keep an air bubble in place.

Most spiders remain with their eggs, looking after them until they have hatched.

Water spiders

Most spiders live on land but a few, such as the water spider, live underwater. It traps air and makes a diving bell, which it anchors to plants.

so quickly that the fly doesn't have a chance to escape

Egg sac

Eggs and babies

Spider's silk is also used to build nests or to attach eggs to the spider to carry around. This spider, however, holds the eggs in her jaws until they hatch.

Become an expert...

on bloodsuckers, pages 116-117
on vampire bats, pages 30-31

Spiders have four pairs of eyes!

Strange land creatures

Apart from insects there
are many creepy crawlies
that run around on land.
Some are large, others
small, some have lots
of legs, and some
no legs at all.

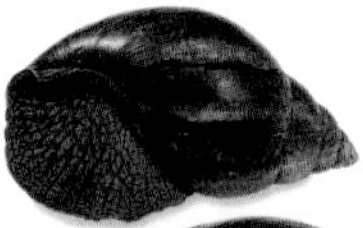

Snails

One of the slowest movers
on land is the snail. When it
feels threatened it doesn't
have to rely on speed,
it simply pulls itself
inside its shell.

The shell of the
snail is attached
to its back.

Snail

A garden snail's shell always
coils in a clockwise direction.

Giant tiger
centipede

Centipedes

The word centipede means
"100 feet", but actually
centipedes have a lot fewer.
Giant tiger centipedes are found
in jungles. They eat spiders
and insects, which they kill
with poison.

How big is the biggest snail in the world?

When pill woodlice are frightened, they curl up into tight balls.

Woodlice

Woodlice may look like insects but they are actually related to crabs and lobsters. They live in dark, damp places to avoid drying up and eat rotten leaves and wood.

Earthworms

Earthworms are long, thin snake-like creatures that live underground. They push their way through the soil eating rotting plants and animals.

Slugs and snails have one muscly foot that they use to walk around on.

Some millipedes roll into balls if they sense danger.

Slug

Millipedes

Millipedes have lots of legs - sometimes as many as 300! But this does not mean they run fast. They have to move their legs in waves to stop them from hitting each other.

Slimy slugs

Slugs are similar to snails but they have no shell. They move by sliding over slime that they squeeze out through their foot. Sometimes they leave a shiny trail behind them.

Slugs spend the day hiding and feed at night.

A leech is a type of worm that sucks blood from animals.

Become an expert...

on sea slugs and sea snails, pages 136-137

133

The Giant African snail can grow to the size of your arm from hand to elbow!

Sea crustaceans

It's easy to see how these creatures got their name – they are covered in hard plates that act like a crust. Most crustaceans live in water.

Crusty creatures

The lobster, like other crustaceans, has a hard skeleton on the outside of its body and two eyes on stalks, called antennae. Lobsters spend their time walking across the sea floor.

Crabs

Crabs are armed with a pair of pincers that can nip very hard when they feel threatened. They live on the sea-shore as well as the sea bed.

Crabs use their pincers to crack the shells of other animals and to pick up food.

The crab's eyes are at the end of these stalks.

Fiddler crab

Some crabs are as big as car tyres!

Which crustacean lives permanently on land?

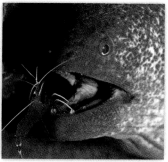

Cleaning up

Some shrimps get their food in a very unusual way – by cleaning the mouths and scales of willing fish. They use their delicate pincers to pick out dead skin and tiny creatures.

Barnacles

On many sea-shores, millions of barnacles cling to rocks. They start life as tiny larvae; when they settle on a rock they fasten themselves to it, grow a hard case around themselves and stay there for life.

Fleshy brown barnacles

Barnacles have wavy legs that catch food in the water.

Red crab alert!

Easter Island in the Pacific Ocean has a community of about 100 million red crabs. Each year at the same time every single crab crosses the island to lay its eggs on the beach. What a traffic jam!

The crabs start walking when the rains come to the island.

Finding a home

Hermit crabs have softer bodies than other crabs, so to protect themselves they hunt for empty shells to live in. Often the crabs fight for a good shell.

Hermit crabs

Become an expert...

on the only land crustacean,
page 133

You are more likely to see woodlice in the garden than on the sea shore.

Sea molluscs

Sea molluscs come in many weird and wonderful shapes. Who would have thought that octopuses and scallops were related? Some live on land, others live in water.

Octopuses are soft creatures with muscly jackets over their bodies

Octopus

Clever clogs

Octopuses and squids have very large brains and are the most intelligent creatures in the creepy crawly section. All octopuses and squids have eight arms.

Octopus relatives

Squids and cuttlefish are the nearest relatives to octopuses.

Blue-ringed octopus: this octopus can change colour and has a nasty bite.

Cuttlefish: these molluscs have eight short arms and two longer tentacles.

Squid: squids are torpedo shaped and can swim very fast indeed.

This octopus has a crab in its jaws.

Become an expert...

on reptiles with shells, pages **84–85**
on land slugs, pages **132–133**

The ink can also numb the enemy stopping it from chasing the octopus or squid further.

Ink squirting

When octopuses and squids feel threatened by another sea creature, they squirt ink out of their bodies to confuse it and act like a smoke screen.

Do octopuses have teeth?

Sea snails

Conches, whelks, and winkles are all sea snails. They have shells and can commonly be seen clinging to rocks. Most eat plants, but some eat other small sea creatures.

Whelk

Sea slugs

Strangely enough, some slugs live under water. Unlike land slugs, sea slugs are very beautiful. Like their cousins, they have no shell, so protect themselves by being poisonous or well camouflaged like this lettuce slug.

Limpets

Limpets have cone-shaped shells that protect them. They cling to rocks and graze on algae, a type of plant, wandering around using their muscular foot.

Each arm is lined with suckers to help it grip to rocks and its prey.

Limpets have been grazing on this rock – you can see the trails they have made.

Limpet

Limpets can often be seen in large clusters on rocks.

Two-hinged shells

Oysters, mussels, scallops, and clams all have a shell that is hinged into two parts that can open and close. They open them to suck food in and breathe, and keep them tightly shut to protect themselves.

Giant clam

Quick scallop

Queen scallops can move surprisingly quickly through the water. They clap the two parts of their shell together and this movement propels them forwards.

The black dots around the shell are eyes.

Queen scallop

No, but they have sharp jaws.

Brainless wonders

The are a lot of very strange sea creatures. Some don't even look like animals at all. The one thing all the animals on these pages have in common is that they have no brains.

Some sponges can grow so big that divers can swim inside them.

The coral reef

Believe it or not coral is an animal, or rather lots of tiny animals stuck together. The skeletons give coral its hard ridges, which provide a home for tiny animals called polyps.

Sponges

Sponges look like plants but are actually animals, even though they are attached to the ground. They are bright colours often making the sea floor look like an underwater garden.

Sea urchin

This spiky creature may look harmless but you wouldn't want to step on one. Sea urchins are covered in sharp spines that protect their soft bodies.

Sea urchins

Sea urchins have tube-shaped feet and can walk across the sea floor.

Become an expert...

on poisonous creatures of the sea, pages 148-149

Which is the most poisonous creature in the sea?

Starfish

Most starfish have five arms that stick out from the centre. They have some strange-looking relations too.

Starfish: almost all starfish look like this one, with five arms.

Sunstar starfish: this starfish is unusual – it has 12 arms.

Grey starfish: this starfish has red nodules all over it.

Brittlestar: it has longer arms than a starfish and moves more easily.

Sea cucumber: this starfish cousin has 8-30 feet around its mouth.

Jellyfish

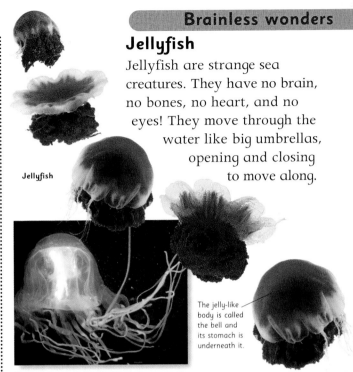

Jellyfish are strange sea creatures. They have no brain, no bones, no heart, and no eyes! They move through the water like big umbrellas, opening and closing to move along.

Jellyfish

The jelly-like body is called the bell and its stomach is underneath it.

The tentacles of the box jellyfish act like fishing lines to catch food.

Sea anemones

Sea anemones look like pretty sea flowers, but they can give lethal stings to small animals. They use their poisonous tentacles to stun fish before they eat them.

Starfish eating mussel

The starfish pushes its stomach through its mouth and into the shell to eat it.

Eating habits

The mouth of a starfish is underneath its body. It uses its arms to crack open mussel shells, then eats up the creature inside.

Sea anemones move across the sea floor by squirting water to jet propel them along.

Dahlia anemones

139

The world of microlife

Some creepy crawlies, whether insects or other tiny creatures, are so small that you can't see them unless you look through a microscope. They are everywhere, however, even in your eyelashes!

Some plankton are as big as your fingernail, others are too small to see.

Unwelcome guests

Tiny animals like to share our body with us. Some are helpful guests but others we would rather get rid of, like this head louse.

Head louse

Eyelash mite

Eyelash mites

Like everyone else in the world, you have had tiny mites living in your eyelashes since you were a baby. They are harmless but can make your eyes itch a little.

Become an expert...

on other creepy-crawly pests and plagues,

pages 116–117

Head lice make your scalp itch.

Some of these tiny bacteria give you a very sick tummy.

140

How many dust mites could you fit in one bed?

A lot of plankton, like this larva, are in fact the babies of many sea creatures.

Sea microlife

The sea is full of microscopic creatures. They are called plankton and there are in fact so many that the sea is like a big, thick plankton soup. Many fish eat the plankton and still there are plenty more.

Plankton

Some huge whales eat only tiny plankton.

Bacteria

There are about 300 types of bacteria that live on your teeth! Although they are technically not animals, they are some of the smallest creatures alive. This is the tip of a needle (magnified many times) and the tiny orange specks are bacteria, or germs. Some of them can make you ill but most are friendly.

House-dust mites

These ferocious-looking creatures are so small that you can't see them. But they are all around you. Dust mites live in your home and love to eat the dead, flaky skin that you shed around the house. Some people are allergic to them.

House-dust mite

Your bed already has about 1 million of them in it!

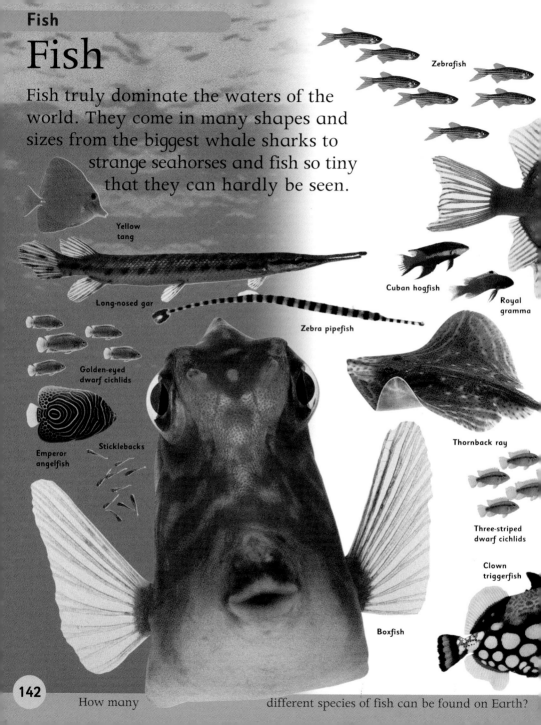

Fish

Fish truly dominate the waters of the world. They come in many shapes and sizes from the biggest whale sharks to strange seahorses and fish so tiny that they can hardly be seen.

Zebrafish

Yellow tang

Long-nosed gar

Cuban hogfish

Royal gramma

Zebra pipefish

Golden-eyed dwarf cichlids

Emperor angelfish

Sticklebacks

Thornback ray

Three-striped dwarf cichlids

Clown triggerfish

Boxfish

How many different species of fish can be found on Earth?

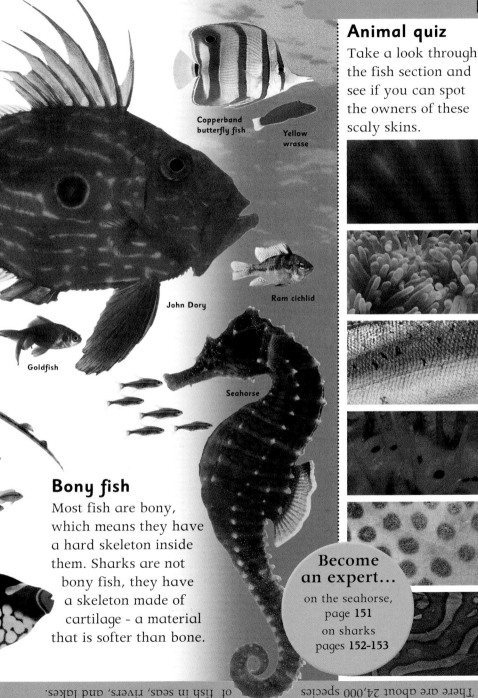

Animal quiz

Take a look through the fish section and see if you can spot the owners of these scaly skins.

Copperband
butterfly fish

Yellow
wrasse

John Dory

Ram cichlid

Goldfish

Seahorse

Bony fish

Most fish are bony, which means they have a hard skeleton inside them. Sharks are not bony fish, they have a skeleton made of cartilage - a material that is softer than bone.

Become an expert...

on the seahorse, page **151**
on sharks
pages **152-153**

There are about 24,000 species of fish in seas, rivers, and lakes.

The world of fish

Fish have been around for 400 million years! They live in seas, rivers, and lakes. Wherever you find water, you can bet there are plenty of fish swimming around.

Types of fish

There are over 24,000 types of fish, which fall into three groups.

Bony fish: 95% of the fish in the world are bony fish with hard skeletons.

Cartilaginous fish: rays, skates, and sharks make up this group.

Jawless fish: only hagfish and lampreys fall into this small group.

Pyjama cardinalfish

Bony fish have a skeleton with a skull, ribs, and a backbone.

Fish skin, made up of scales, is slimy to let them slip through water easily.

The gills lie behind the eyes.

Fish have fins that keep them upright when they swim.

The tail of a fish sweeps from side to side to push the fish forwards.

Gills

Like other animals, fish need to take in oxygen in order to live. But, unlike us, they can breathe underwater using their gills. Fish gulp in water and their gills filter the oxygen out of it.

Mudskipper

Fish out of water

Mudskippers are one of the only fish that can survive out of water. They have special gills that take oxygen from air or water. They skip along mudflats using their fins as elbows.

Which fish is the slowcoach of the sea?

The art of swimming

Many fish swim like snakes slide – they wriggle in an 's' shape. Their whole bodies move from side to side and their tails flick to push them forwards. Their fins help to steer them.

Scales

Most fish are covered in hundreds of scales that overlap like roof tiles. Tiny animals can get under the scales and harm them, so fish let others give them a regular clean.

Some fish can turn on their sides and roll right over. A few can even swim upside-down!

Mandarin fish

Colours can be used for camouflage or to attract a mate.

Carp

Colour

Fish come in all colours and patterns. Freshwater fish and those living in cooler waters tend to be duller in colour. Tropical fish are sometimes incredibly bright and beautiful.

Eels are found in fresh water and sea water.

Living together

Fish sometimes live in huge groups called shoals. When so many swim together they look like one big fish so they are less likely to be attacked.

Fishy features

Most fish look like the pyjama cardinalfish on the left. Some however have a different appearance. This eel looks more like a snake with fins. Unlike a snake it has sharp teeth.

The seahorse is the slowest fish that lives in the sea.

Finding food

Most fish are meat eaters, which means everyone is eating everyone in the water. It's a very dangerous place.

Electric eel
This eel has three electric organs in its body. It catches prey by giving them electric shocks. These can stun or kill a fish and put a human into hospital!

Fish eat fish
The sea is one great big food chain. Plankton are eaten by small fish and big fish eat them.

Plankton: plankton contains tiny sea fish that live near the surface.

Herring: small fish like herring like to eat the tiny plankton.

Salmon: larger fish, such as salmon, eat the smaller fish, and they get eaten by sharks!

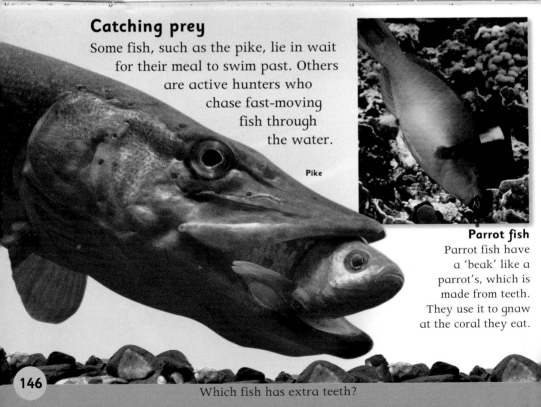

Catching prey
Some fish, such as the pike, lie in wait for their meal to swim past. Others are active hunters who chase fast-moving fish through the water.

Pike

Parrot fish
Parrot fish have a 'beak' like a parrot's, which is made from teeth. They use it to gnaw at the coral they eat.

Which fish has extra teeth?

Fish are attracted to the glowing bait that sits right by its mouth.

The angler fish

The angler fish does what fishermen do. Attached to its head is a glowing "rod and bait" that attracts small fish. When one of them gets close, it gets gobbled up!

Archerfish can snap insects out of the air.

Archerfish

Become an expert...

on the ultimate meat eaters of the sea – sharks, pages 152-153

Leaping fish!

Most fish feed in water, but a few can catch food out of water too. The archerfish leaps into the air and picks insects off overhanging branches.

An experienced adult can shoot a stem of water four times its own length.

Piranhas

Piranhas have a fearsome reputation. Their razor sharp teeth can strip the flesh from animals in minutes. Piranhas eat fruit and seeds as well as living things.

Piranhas work in groups to tear creatures to pieces.

Piranhas

It is extremely dangerous for animals, humans included, to swim in water filled with piranhas.

The deep-sea viperfish has extra teeth in its throat to help push its food down.

Staying alive

So many water creatures feed on fish that they all have to be careful – or very cunning – to make sure they don't get eaten.

Porcupine fish

The flat porcupine fish looks like any other fish in the tropical seas.

Ballooning up

The porcupine fish seems harmless until it is alarmed. It then gulps in water to blow itself up, which pushes out its spines making it impossible to swallow.

Safety in numbers

Fish that live in shoals, or groups, are far safer in large numbers. They all keep an eye out for enemies and will sometimes split into two groups to confuse them.

Camouflage

Many fish use camouflage to hide. Flatfish, such as this plaice, bury themselves on the sea floor, then change their colour to blend into the sand and the stones.

What is the most poisonous fish in the world for a human to eat?

The bright stripes on a lionfish warn other creatures off: the poison in its fins can kill a human.

Twinspot wrasse

The con artist
The twinspot wrasse tries to fool its enemies. There are two big spots on its body that look like eyes. It buries itself in the sand and just shows the spots, making it look like a large, frightening fish.

Poison
The bright colouring of some poisonous fish tells the predators that they would not make a tasty meal. This spiky lionfish, is one of the most poisonous fish in the sea.

Lionfish

Friend or foe?
These clownfish use poisonous sea anemones for protection; the poison doesn't seem to affect the fish, who dive in when danger approaches.

Clownfish

Become an expert...
on insect defence, pages 114-115

Hidey holes
Garden eels dig holes in the sand. During the day they hang out looking like a field of sea grass catching small fish. When threatened they dive back into their holes.

The pufferfish.

Making more fish

Most fish don't make very good parents – they lay their eggs in the water and abandon them, leaving their young to fend for themselves. Some, however, do stick around.

Baby sticklebacks

Courting

Some male fish make more of an effort to attract a female than others. The male stickleback builds a nest, then his tummy turns red to attract a female.

The male stickleback guards his eggs until they hatch.

Millions of eggs

Most fish lay eggs. The perch, like many other fish, lays an enormous number in the hope that some will hatch out. A lot of other fish like to eat the eggs so most will be lost.

A good father

The bullhead male is a keen parent. The female lays only a few hundred eggs and the male guards them fiercely until they hatch.

Hatching out

Most fish hatch into tiny larvae – fish that are not quite formed. They gradually grow a skeleton, fins, and organs. At this small stage they can't protect themselves easily.

Which fish lays the most eggs?

When the male wants to eat, he spits the eggs out.

Become an expert...
on other animals that lay their eggs in the water,
pages **98-99**

The ultimate protection

The yellowhead jawfish father has a foolproof way to protect his eggs. When the female has laid them, he keeps them inside his mouth until they hatch.

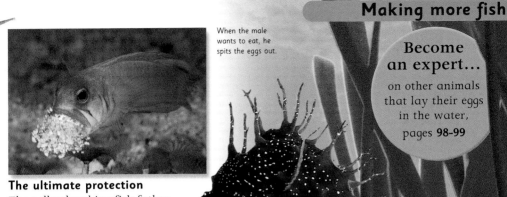

The father seahorse keeps the babies inside his pouch until they can defend themselves.

Seahorses

A seahorse keeps itself in one position by wrapping its tail around a plant.

Seahorses

The seahorse is very unusual indeed – the female lays the eggs inside a pouch on the male's tummy and then the male gives birth to the babies!

The incredible journey

Some fish have a special place where they lay their eggs. The salmon lives in the sea but travels as far as 1,500 km (1,000 miles) up rivers to lay its eggs in the same place it was born. It even swims up waterfalls to get there.

The ocean sunfish can lay a staggering 30 million eggs in one go.

Shark types

There are many different families of sharks. Some look very different to the common torpedo shape.

Leopard shark: it has golden spotted skin that camouflages it well.

Saw shark: its long nose has razor-sharp teeth down it, like a saw.

Hammerhead: this shark has a rectangular head with eyes at each end.

Wobbegong: it has weedy flaps around its nose for camouflage.

Many people think that great whites are the most dangerous animals in the sea, but they rarely attack humans.

Great white shark

Sharks and rays

A shark's fin poking out of the water is enough to send a chill down your spine. But they also fill fish with fear – sharks are the largest and most successful meat-eaters of the sea.

Bendy bones

Sharks and rays do not have bones. Instead their skeleton is made of soft, bendy cartilage – the same stuff that's in your nose and ears.

Black-tipped reef shark

Born in a purse

Some sharks start life as a tiny adult in an egg case, which looks a bit like a handbag. This case is attached to seaweed and the baby shark grows inside for about 6-9 months.

Egg case

Empty egg cases are known as mermaid's purses.

A lethal smile

The massive jaws of the great white shark contain a terrifying set of sharp teeth, which often fall out as they tear flesh. A shark may lose 30,000 teeth in a lifetime. They are, however, always replaced with new sharp ones.

What is the largest fish in the world?

The gentle giant

Although all sharks eat meat, not all of them eat big prey. This basking shark is an underwater giant but eats only the tiniest creatures. It gulps huge amounts of water and filters tiny animal plankton from it.

Rays' mouths are underneath their bodies. They have very strong teeth to crush shells with.

Rays

Rays are sharks' cousins, but unlike their relatives, they are flat, and live mostly on the sea-bed, in shallow, warm water.

Rays swim by flapping their side fins just like wings.

Spotted ray

Become an expert...

on other large sea animals that feed by filtering tiny animals, pages **46-47**

Spot the eyes

Most rays are coloured to match the sea-bed, but they also bury into the sand for extra camouflage. Blue spotted stingrays bury themselves with just their eyes showing when they rest.

Some rays, such as stingrays, have spines on their tails that can sting a predator.

Monster of the deep

The manta ray is the monster in the family, sometimes stretching 6 m (20 ft) across – that's almost the length of a bus! Some swim in small shoals, but most live alone.

The whale shark is the biggest fish in the world.

Amazing animal facts

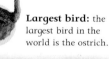

The mosquito is the most dangerous animal on Earth to humans. It carries a deadly diseases called malaria.

Malaria kills up to 2 million people every year.

Reptiles and amphibians

This section can claim the oldest animals in the world and some of the most poisonous too.

Largest reptile: the saltwater crocodile can be up to 7 m (23 ft) long.

Oldest reptile: there has been one tortoise who lived for 150 years!

Deadliest snake: the carpet viper is responsible for the most human deaths.

Largest toad: the cane toad would sit happily on a dinner plate – and fill it.

Largest amphibian: the giant salamander is as big as an average man.

Mammals

The mammal section includes the largest, loudest, and tallest animals in the world.

Largest land animal: the African bull elephant is the largest land animal.

Dullest eater: the koala has a very dull diet. It only eats eucalyptus.

Loudest land animal: the loudest animal is the howler monkey.

Tallest animal: the tallest animal on Earth is the giraffe.

Birds

The bird section contains the true record breakers of the flying world.

Largest wingspan: the widest bird is the wandering albatross.

Smallest bird: the tiniest bird is the bee hummingbird.

Fastest diver: the fastest air diver is the peregrine falcon.

Largest bird: the largest bird in the world is the ostrich.

The cheetah is the

What is the rarest large land mammal in the world?

Creepy crawlies

The creepy crawly section contains some of the most extraordinary-looking animals on Earth.

The three-toed sloth of South America is the slowest mammal on Earth.

This sloth has an average ground speed of 2 m (7 ft) per minute. But in the trees it can double that speed.

Largest moth: The atlas moth is often mistaken for a bird. It is 30 cm (12 in) wide.

Biggest eye: the largest eye in relation to the animal belongs to the giant squid.

Largest spider: the Goliath bird-eating spider would easily cover a plate.

Most legs: the animal with the most legs is the millipede – some have 750!

Fish

Fish dominate the water world – and the majority of the Earth is covered in water.

Most fish eggs: the ocean sunfish can lay 30 million eggs at one spawning.

Largest fish: the whale shark is the largest fish in the world.

Largest freshwater fish: the European catfish is the largest freshwater fish.

Prickliest fish: as well as spines, porcupine fish also have sharp teeth.

Fastest fish: the sailfish can swim faster than the cheetah can run (see below).

fastest-running animal on Earth

Cheetahs run amazingly fast. When they are chasing prey on level ground, they can reach speeds of over 100km/h (62 mph) in short bursts.

The Javan rhinoceros, of which there are only 70 left.

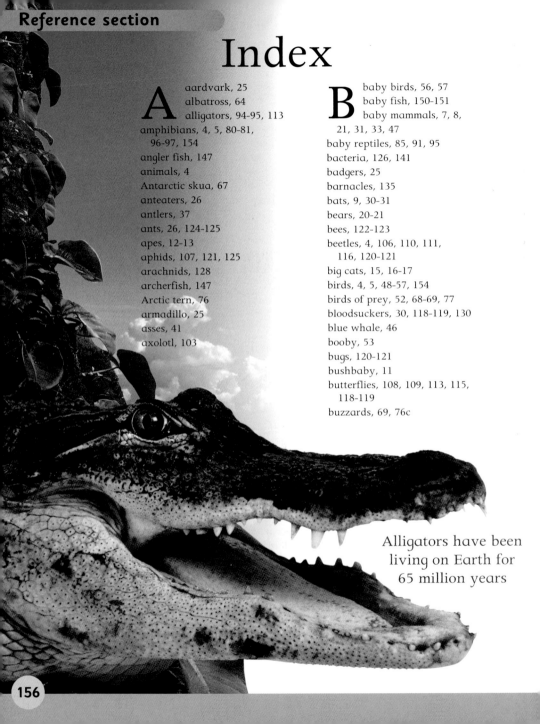

Index

Alligators have been
living on Earth for
65 million years

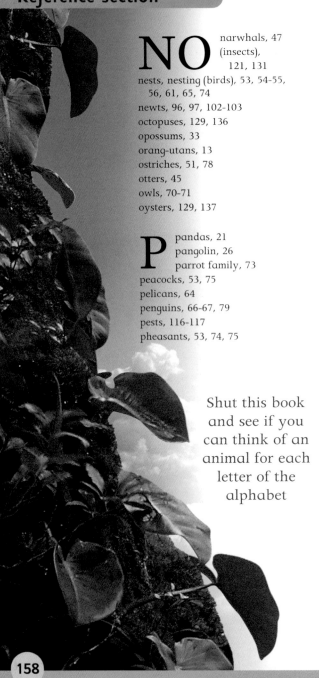

Shut this book
and see if you
can think of an
animal for each
letter of the
alphabet

There are three
different families
of zebras. They
all have slightly
different stripe
patterns and
colours

Picture credits

The publisher would like to thank the following for their kind permission to reproduce their photographs:

(Key: a-above; c-centre; b-below; l-left; r-right; t-top)

Alamy Images: Photo 24/Brand X Pictures 12tl; Byron Schumaker 121r; D. Robert Franz/Imagestate 18br; Esa Hiltula 19cl; Focus Group/Lynne Siler 42cr; Marin Harvey 12b; Mark Hamblin 19tl; Mark J. Barrett 40l; Maximilian Weinzierl 121ca; Paul Horsted/Stock Connection, Inc 91cbr; Steve Bloom Images 13r; Tom Brakefield/Stock Connection Inc 32-33b. **Ardea London Ltd**: 53tc; Becca Saunders 152claa; Chris Knights 69crb, 74clb; D. Parer & E. Parer-Cook 46tr; Donald D. Burgess 55tr; G. Robertson 66tr, 67tr; Jean Paul Ferrero 41tr, 133tr, 134-135cb; Joanna Van Gruisen 154cr; John Cancalosi 54br; Kenneth W. Fink 13b, 21clb, 72bl; M. Watson 54tr, 95cla; Pat Morris 25tr, 97cr, 124tr, 146ca; Peter Steyn 87cr; Stefan Meyers 52-53bs; Steve Hopkin 115tl; Valerie Taylor 139c, 146cr, 155cb. **Corbis**: 72-73bc; Anthony Bannister; Gallo Images 107c, 130cr, 150br; Bohemian Nomad Picturemakers 155br; Bryan Knox; Papilio 123bl; Buddy Mays 155tr; Carol Hughes; Gallo Images 106b; Chase Swift 37c; Chinch Gryniewicz; Ecoscene 131c; D. Robert & Lorri Franz 9tr; Dan Guravich 119tc; David A. Northcott 154-155b; Douglas Faulkner 44-45c; Douglas P. Wilson; Frank Lane Picture Agency 140tr, 141tl, 141cr; Fritz Polking; Frank Lane Picture Agency 113clb; Galen Rowell 9r; George D. Lepp 118br; Herb Watson 4cla; Joe McDonald 9bc, 30tl, 99tr; Karl Ammann 41cl; Kennan Ward 46crb; Kevin Schafer 10tr; Lynda Richardson 123cb; Martin Harvey 33br, 85cr; Mary Ann McDonald 22tl; Michael & Patricia Fogden 52cl, 94tr; Paul A. Souders 51cr, 124-125b; Paul Funston; Gallo Images 106cl; Peter Johnson 124cl; Tim Davis 21tr; Tom Nebbia 78-79b; W. Perry Conway 28br, 29tr, 33t; Wolfgang Kaehler 53cr, 53bl, 79cr. **DK Images**: Andy Crawford and Kit Houghton 36tr; Barnabas Kindersley 64bl; Barrie Watts 29bl, 56bl; Franklin Park Zoo 8ca; Gables 68cr; Jane Burton 61bc; Jerry Young 53tl, 63cr, 63crb, 64bc, 74-75bc, 76crbb, 79cl, 80cbl, 84clb, 85cla, 85cl, 101clb, 101clb, 110cr, 130tl, 130bl, 143tc; Kim Taylor 58cr; Mike Linley 100cr; NASA 70tc; Natural History Museum 4r, 47craa, 50bcl, cbl, 51clb, 55bc, bccr, bcr, 55cla, claa, 71cb, 74bc, 84cl, 118tr, 118cra, 118cl, 118car, 118cbl, 120crb, 121clb, 121bl, 135tr; Paignton Zoo 39tc; Paradise Park Cornwall 78tr; Philip Dowell 79tr; Philip Enticknap 76crb; University College 8tl; Weymouth Sea Life Centre 139cl. **Getty Images**: Cousteau Society 145cbr; David Nardini 148l; Douglas D. Seifert 153b; Georgette Douwma 145r; JH Pete Carmichael 91t; John Downer 35br; Natalie Fobes 151bl; Peter David 147tl; Tim Davis 66l. **Robert Harding Picture Library**: 92ca. **Image Quest Marine**: Carlos Villoch 151tl; James D. Watt 138l, 152cla; Nat Sumanatemeya 135tl; Scott Tuason 138cr. **FLPA - Images of Nature**: David Hosking 63tr; G Moon 77cl; Mike Jones 57clb; Minden Pictures 64cl, 64br, 77t; S. Charlie Brown 61clb; S Maslowski 62bl; Steve Young 65cl. **Masterfile UK**: Albert Normandin 40-41b. **National Geographic Image Collection**: Bill Curtsinger 84c; J. Eastcott/Y.Eastcott Film 20cr; Raymond Gehman 94bl; Robert Madden 59cl; Roy Toft 20-21b; Tim Laman 101r. **Nature Picture Library Ltd**: Alan James 153tl; Anup Shah 95br; Brandon Cole 152bl; Bruce Davidson 120c; Conrad Mauf 89c; Dan Burton 133tl; Fabio Liverani 103cr; Georgette Douwma 145tl; Jurgen Freund 91clb; Pat de la Harpe 95tr. **N.H.P.A.**: Andy Rouse 9clbb, 16cr, 17tl, 17cl, 36crb, 46-47b; Ann & Steve Toon 16bl, 23br; Ant Photo Library 33cb, 125br; Anthony Bannister 24-25, 92-93cb, 111tr; B Jones & M Shimlock 47bc, 149bl; Christophe Ratier 78cr; Dan Griggs 114cb; Daniel Heuclin 26tr, 27c, 32tr, 96cra, 97crb, 154br; David & Irene Myers 46cl; E A Janes 39bl; Eric Soder 14l; G.I Bernard 116crb; Gerard Lacz 23clb, 45bl; Hellio & Van Ingen 37tl, 117tl; Henry Ausloos 18bl; J & A Scott 9tl, 16-17b, 38ca; James Warwick 70cr; Jany Sauvanet 26bl, 147clb; John Buckingham 98bc; John Shaw 14bc, 23bl, 75br; Karl Switak 90cl; Kevin Schafer 11tr, 54, 67b; Laurie Campbell 65r, 82bl; LUTRA 146bl, 150cla; Manfred Danegger 24bc; Marin Wendler 15br; Mark Bowler 42tr; Martin Harvey 15bl, 34cl; Martin Wendler 93clb; Melvin Grey 57r; Mirko Stelzner 73r; Nick Garbutt 10bl, 36bl; Norbert Wu 45tr; Rich Kirchner 67c; Rod Planck 117b; Roger Tidman 31t; Stephen Dalton 11br, 23clbb, 30br, 30-31c, 31br, 60br, 61cr, 71t, 87tl, 87clb, 101tl, 103bl, 120bl, 122l, 126-127b, 130cra, 131br; Stephen Krasemann 43cl; T Kitchin & V Hurst 22tr. **Oxford Scientific Films**: 35tc, 113br, 131c; Adam Jones 62-63b; Alan Root/SAL 26crb; Bert & Babs Wells 32cra; Bob Bennett 39cla; Brian Kenney 13tl, 112tr; Carol Farneti Foster 14cra; Clive Bromhall 13c; Daniel Cox 18tl, 65tl; F. Polking/OKAPIA 62bc; Frank Schneidermeyer 15tr; James H Robinson 112br; Javed Jaffeji 23ca; John Downer 76-77b; John Forsdyke 116br; Jorge Sierra Antinolo 10c; Judd Cooney 77cb; Kim Kesterskov 64t, 154c; Leonard Lee Rue 11tl; Lon E Lauber 76cra; London Scientific Films 108l; Mark Hamblin 37bl, 65br; Michael Dick/AA 10cr; Michael Fogden 60c, 89bl; Michael H. Francis/OKAPIA 40crb; Mike Powles 43cr; Paolo Fioratti 39clbb; Partridge Films Ltd 31cr; Patti Murray/AA 115cl; Paulo de Oliveira 36cla; Peter Hawkey/SAL 76ca; Richard Packwood 38tr; Rob Nunnington 39tr; Robert Tyrell 60bl, 154cb; Roger Brown 32cr; Satoschi Kuribayashi 121tl; Stan Osolinski 11bl, 37c, 38-39b, 42c; Thomas Haider 44l; Tom Ulrich 39clb, 39claa; Wendy Shattil and Bob Rozinski 23tl; Zig Leszczynski/AA 47tl. **Science Photo Library**: 140cr, 140bl; Dr Tony Brain 141bl; Eye of Science 127c, 141br; Rod Planck 25bl. **Still Pictures**: James Gerholdt 99cr; Klein 32c; Martin Harvey 42-43b.

All other images © Dorling Kindersley
www.dkimages.com

Acknowledgements

Dorling Kindersley would like to thank: Ben Morgan for his extensive knowledge on the subject, Lynn Bresler for compiling the index, Lorrie Mack for proof-reading, and Janet Allis, Cathy Chesson, Jacqueline Gooden, and Cheryl Telfer for design assistance.